The Dale Carnegie Code

Dale Harbison Carnegie was an American writer and the developer of famous courses in self-development, salesmanship, corporate training, public speaking and interpersonal skills. He is the author of the bestselling *How to Win Friends and Influence People*, *How to Stop Worrying and Start Living* and many more self-help books.

The Dale Carnegie Code

Unlocking the ***Power*** of ***People Skills*** and ***Lasting Relationships***

Dale Carnegie

RUPA

Published by
Rupa Publications India Pvt. Ltd 2024
7/16, Ansari Road, Daryaganj
New Delhi 110002

Sales centres:
Bengaluru Chennai
Hyderabad Jaipur Kathmandu
Kolkata Mumbai Prayagraj

P-ISBN: 978-93-5702-977-3
E-ISBN: 978-93-5702-769-4

Second impression 2024

10 9 8 7 6 5 4 3 2

Printed in India

CONTENTS

1. How to Make People Like You Instantly 7
2. Starting to Communicate 10
3. Increase Courage and Self-Confidence 17
4. Do This and You'll Be Welcome Anywhere 25
5. Make a Good First Impression 31
6. Expressing Genuine Interest in Others 36
7. Listening to Learn 40
8. The Truth About Gesture 49
9. No One Likes to Take Orders 61
10. "If You Want to Gather Honey, Don't Kick Over the Beehive" 64
11. How to Interest Your Audience 71
12. Seeing Things from the Other Person's Point of View 89
13. How to Deal with People 100
14. After-Dinner and Other Occasional Speaking 109
15. A Sure Way of Making Enemies—and How to Avoid It 111
16. A Magic Formula 121

17. The Talk to Convince 130
18. Voice Charm 144
19. Put a "Stop-Loss" Order on Your Worries 149
20. If You Must Find Fault, This Is the Way to Begin 154
21. Talk About Your Own Mistakes First 161
22. How to Criticize—and Not Be Hated for It 163
23. A Drop of Honey 167

1

HOW TO MAKE PEOPLE LIKE YOU INSTANTLY

There is one all-important law of human conduct. If we obey that law, we shall almost never get into trouble. In fact, that law, if obeyed, will bring us countless friends and constant happiness. But the very instant we break the law, we shall get into endless trouble. The law is this: *Always make the other person feel important.* John Dewey, as we have already noted, said that the desire to be important is the deepest urge in human nature; and William James said: "The deepest principle in human nature is the craving to be appreciated." As I have already pointed out, it is this urge that differentiates us from the animals. It is this urge that has been responsible for civilization itself.

Philosophers have been speculating on the rules of human relationships for thousands of years, and out of all that speculation, there has evolved only one important precept. It is not new. It is as old as history. Zoroaster taught it to his followers in Persia 2,500 years ago. Confucius preached it in China 24 centuries ago. Lao-tse, the founder of Taoism, taught it to his disciples in the Valley of the Han. Buddha preached it on the bank of the Holy Ganges 500 years before Christ. The sacred books of Hinduism taught it among the stony hills of Judea 19 centuries ago. Jesus summed it up in one thought—probably the most important rule in the world: "Do unto others as you would have others do unto you."

You want the approval of those with whom you come in contact. You want recognition of your true worth. You want a feeling that you are important in your little world. You don't want to listen to cheap, insincere flattery, but you do crave sincere appreciation. You want your friends and associates to be, as Charles Schwab put it, "hearty in their approbation and lavish in their praise." All of us want that.

So let's obey the Golden Rule, and give unto others what we would have others give unto us.

THE PHILOSOPHY OF APPRECIATION

How? When? Where? The answer is: All the time, everywhere.

You don't have to wait until you are ambassador to France or chairman of the Clambake Committee of your lodge before you use this philosophy of appreciation. You can work magic with it almost every day.

If, for example, the waitress brings us mashed potatoes when we have ordered French fries, let's say, "I'm sorry to trouble you, but I prefer the French fries." She'll probably reply, "No trouble at all" and will be glad to change the potatoes, because we have shown respect for her.

Little phrases such as "I'm sorry to trouble you," "Would you be so kind as to—?" "Won't you please?" "Would you mind?" "Thank you"—little courtesies like these oil the cogs of the monotonous grind of everyday life—and incidentally, they are the hallmark of good breeding.

POINTS TO REMEMBER

1. Always make the other person feel important.
2. Act with others how you want them to act with you.
3. Old magic words will save the day.

2

STARTING TO COMMUNICATE

Nothing could be easier than failing to communicate. Condescending, contradicting, berating, demeaning, treating other people as if "I am the boss, and you just work here"—until recently these were widely accepted forms of human interaction inside some of the largest and best-known companies in the world. "Barking rights" were thought to be a natural prerogative of executive positions, along with an office window and a two-hour lunch. Families, schools, and other organizations unfortunately followed suit.

For years loudness was equated with toughness. Stubbornness was equated with superior knowledge. Argumentativeness was equated with honesty. We should all—supervisor and employee, parent and child, teacher and student—be grateful those days are finally coming to an end.

More and more people, in businesses and elsewhere, are beginning to understand how important good communication really is. The ability to communicate well is what lights the fire in people. It's what turns great ideas into action. It's what makes all achievement possible.

Communicating well is not terribly complicated—not in theory, anyway. Communicating, after all, is something every one of us does every day in our personal lives. We've all been communicating since the early days of childhood. At least we think we have. But true communication, effective communication, is in fact relatively rare in the adult world.

START FROM THE BASICS

There's no secret recipe for learning to communicate well, but there are some basic concepts that can be mastered with relative ease. Here are the first steps to successful communication.

Follow them and you will be on your way.

1. Make communication a top priority.
2. Be open to other people.
3. Create a receptive environment for communication.

No matter how busy you find yourself during the work day, *you absolutely must make time to communicate.* All the brilliant ideas in the world are worthless if you don't share them. Communication can be accomplished in many ways—in meetings, in face-to-face sessions with colleagues, just walking down the hall, or stopping at the water cooler, or spending half an hour in the company lunchroom. What's most important is that communicating never stop. The need for effective communication doesn't stop at the office door. It extends to the home, to the school, to the church, even to the halls of science. Any place where people meet with people, communication is key.

It used to be that research scientists could spend their whole lives in the laboratory, singlemindedly searching for the truths of the natural order. But those days are gone. In today's competitive world, even scientists need to listen and talk.

"Many scientists don't know how to effectively communicate what they are doing," says Dr. Ronald M. Evans, an eminent research professor at the Salk Institute for Biological Studies. "They know what they are doing. They have a pretty good idea of why they're doing it. But they have difficulty putting that into perspective, transmitting the ideas outside the laboratory. It's a major limitation at many levels. To obtain funding, you have to convince people that you're doing something that's important."

When Lee Iacocca first went to work at the Ford Motor Company, he discovered the same limitation in many automobile designers and engineers: "I've known a lot of engineers with terrific ideas who had trouble explaining them to other people. It's always a shame when a guy with great talent can't tell the board or a committee what's in his head."

Without mastery of that very basic human skill—the ability to talk and listen to others—members of a company, a school, or a family can't thrive for long.

The biggest mistake managers used to make—besides thinking that all wisdom flowed from them—was failing to understand that communication absolutely has to be a two-way street. You have to share your ideas with others and listen to theirs. That's step number two: *Be open to other people—above, below, and beside.*

Publilius Syrus, the Roman playwright, recognized this fact of human nature two thousand years ago. "We are interested in others when they are interested in us," Syrus wrote.

If you can show your colleagues you are receptive to their ideas, they're more likely to be receptive to yours—and to keep you honestly informed about the things you need to know. Show that you care about the future of the organization and that you care as much about them. And don't limit those displays of concern to your coworkers. Communicate the same genuine caring to your customers and your clients too.

At Saunders Karp & Company, merchant banker Thomas A. Saunders III spends his professional life looking for growing companies to invest his clients' funds in. He's an expert at spotting business gems. Nothing impresses Saunders more than a company that really knows how to communicate with its customers.

He recently paid a visit to a wholesale jewelry company in Lafayette, Louisiana. He spent a day touring the company's facilities. But all it really took was five minutes in the telemarketing room for Saunders to recognize a first-string communications success.

"They handled their customers very efficiently on the phone, and the quality of the service was extremely high," Saunders said. "They didn't seem to make any mistakes. It was just bing, bing, bing, 'You want this?... Yes, we have that in stock... You want two of those, fine... You want three of those, fine... Yes, we have them... No, you have to back-order that... May I suggest a substitution?... Yes, well, if you look on page six hundred of our catalog, there's a mounting...' Boom. 'Thank you very much.' It was over in fifteen seconds. Unbelievable."

The average call took fifteen seconds, and the average customer went away thrilled. Who wouldn't put money in a company like that?

It's easy to become isolated from customers and colleagues, especially for those people who rise in an organization. But no matter how high you get, communication still has to run in all directions, talking and listening, up, down, and around the chain of command.

Ronald Reagan wasn't called the Great Communicator for nothing. Throughout his long political career he made it a point to listen and talk to the people he served. Even when he was president, Reagan continued to read constituent mail. He would have his White House secretaries give him a selection of letters each afternoon. At night he would take them up to his quarters and write out personal replies.

Bill Clinton has put the televised town meeting to much the same use: keeping himself informed about how people are feeling and showing people that he cares about them. Even if he doesn't have solutions for all the problems they bring up, there Clinton is, listening, connecting, articulating his own ideas.

There's nothing new about any of this. Abraham Lincoln took a similar approach more than a century ago. In those days, any citizen could petition the president. Sometimes Lincoln would ask an aide to respond, but frequently he would answer the petitioners personally.

He took some criticism for that. Why bother when there was a war to be fought, a union to be saved? Because Lincoln knew that understanding public opinion was an essential part of being president, and he wanted to hear it firsthand.

Richard L. Fenstermacher, executive director of North American auto operations marketing at Ford Motor Company, is a firm believer in that. "My door's open," he's constantly telling his people. "If you're walking up the hall and you see me in there, even if you just want to say hi, stop in. If you want to bounce an idea off me, do it. Don't feel you have to go through the managers."

That kind of easy interaction doesn't happen by accident. That's where rule number three comes into play: *Create a receptive environment for communication.*

GOOD COMMUNICATION THRIVES AT A HEALTHY WORK ENVIRONMENT

It's a basic fact about communicating with people: they won't say what they think—and won't listen receptively to what you say—unless a foundation of genuine trust and shared interest has been laid. You can't be insincere. How you really feel about communication, whether you're open or not, comes through loud and clear, no matter what you say. "You know right away if somebody is approachable or if they're not," Olympic gymnast Mary Lou Retton has said. "When you get that feeling, you can read a person by nonverbal communication and body language. You know when somebody is standing in the corner and saying, 'Hey, I don't want to be talked to.'"

How can you avoid sending that message? Be open, like people, and let them know you do. Follow Retton's advice: "Being down-to-earth and humble is extremely important. I just try to put people at ease. Everybody's the same. I think everybody is on a certain level, whether you are the CEO of a company or a salesperson. It's just a different job." That's what creating a receptive environment is all about: putting people at ease.

It used to be easier than it is today. Television announcer and former baseball great Joe Garagiola remembers how much one-on-one contact there used to be between the players and the fans: "When we used to come off the field and go to our homes after the games, we would ride the subways with the same fans who were in the stands a few hours earlier.

"It wasn't uncommon for one of the fans to say, 'Hey, Joe, why did you swing at that third strike? Why didn't you let it go?' Now there isn't the same personal connection between the fan and the players other than reading about whether or not he's signing a six- or a seven-million-dollar contract."

One last thing to remember: *Once people do take the risk of telling you what they think, don't punish them for their openness. Do nothing—absolutely nothing—to discourage them from taking the risk of communicating again.*

"If an employee makes a suggestion that I don't agree with, then I have to be very delicate about the way in which I tell them I don't agree," says Fred J. Sievert, chief financial officer of the New York Life Insurance Company. "I want to encourage them to come back to me the next time and make another suggestion. Now, I told some of the people on my staff that I may disagree with them ninety-nine times out of a hundred, but I want them to keep coming to me with their views. That's what they get paid for. The one time out of a hundred is going to be of value, and I'm not going to view them as any weaker because I disagree with them the other times."

One in a hundred. That may not sound so impressive, but great fortunes have been made on odds less certain than that. That's why listening and sharing ideas is so important.

The truth of the matter is that communication is both a skill and an art. It's a process worth thinking about and practicing more than most people do. It sometimes involves showing personal vulnerability by putting your ideas on the line. You're sharing with others and asking them to share with you. That's not always easy. It takes work and time. Techniques have to be acquired and practiced constantly. But take heart. Practice does make perfect, or very nearly so.

POINTS TO REMEMBER

1. Good ideas turn out to be great ideas through communication.
2. Communication is a two-way street between an employer and employee.
3. A nurturing environment is crucial for healthy communication.

3

INCREASE COURAGE AND SELF-CONFIDENCE

The gaining of self-confidence and courage and the ability to think calmly and clearly while talking to a group is not one-tenth as difficult as most men imagine. It is not a gift bestowed by Providence on only a few rarely endowed individuals. It is like the ability to play golf. Any man can develop his own latent capacity if he has sufficient desire to do so.

Is there the faintest shadow of a reason why you should not be able to think as well in a perpendicular position before an audience as you can when sitting down? Surely, you know there is not. In fact, you ought to think better when facing a group of men. Their presence ought to stir you and lift you. A great many speakers will tell you that the presence of an audience is a stimulus, an inspiration, that drives their brains to function more clearly, more keenly. At such times, thoughts, facts, ideas, that they did not know they possessed, drift smoking by, as Henry Ward Beecher said; and they have but to reach out and lay their hands hot upon them. They ought to be your experience. It probably will be if you practice and persevere.

Of this much, however, you may be absolutely sure: training

and practice will wear away your audience-fright and give you self-confidence and an abiding courage.

Do not imagine that your case is unusually difficult. Even those who afterwards became the most eloquent representatives of their generation were, at the outset of their careers, afflicted by this blinding fear and self-consciousness.

Some men, no matter how often they speak, always experience this self-consciousness just before they commence; but in a few seconds after they have got on their feet, it disappears.

Even Lincoln felt shy for the few opening moments. In a few moments he gained composure and warmth and earnestness, and his real speech began.

Your experience may be similar to his.

THE PRE-REQUISITES

In order to get the most out of this training, and to get it with rapidity and dispatch, four things are essential:

First: Start with a Strong and Persistent Desire

This is of far more importance than you probably realize. If your instructor could look into your mind and heart now and ascertain the depth of your desires, he could foretell, almost with certainty, the swiftness of the progress you will make. If your desire is pale and flabby, your achievements will also take on that hue and consistency. But, if you go after this subject with persistence, and with the energy of a bulldog after a cat, nothing underneath the Milky Way will defeat you.

Therefore, arouse your enthusiasm for this study. Enumerate its benefits. Think of what additional self-confidence and the ability to talk more convincingly in business will mean to you. Think of what it may mean to you socially; of the friends it will bring, of the increase of your personal influence, of the leadership it will give you. And it will give you leadership more rapidly than almost any other activity you can think of or imagine.

It is an attainment that almost every person of education longs for. After Andrew Carnegie's death there was found, among his papers, a plan for his life drawn up when he was thirty-three years of age. He then felt that in two more years he could so arrange his business as to have an annual income of fifty thousand dollars; so he proposed to retire at thirty-five, go to Oxford and get a thorough education, and *"pay special attention to speaking in public."*

Think of the glow of satisfaction and pleasure that will accrue from the exercise of this new power. I have traveled round over no small part of this terrestrial ball; and have had many and varied experiences; but for downright, and lasting inward satisfaction, I know of few things that will compare to standing before an audience and making men think your thoughts after you. It will give you a sense of strength, a feeling of power. It will appeal to your pride of personal accomplishment. It will set you off from and raise you above your fellowmen. There is magic in it and a never-to-be-forgotten thrill. "Two minutes before I begin," a speaker confessed, "I would rather be whipped than start; but two minutes before I finish, I would rather be shot than stop."

In every course, some men grow faint-hearted and fall by the wayside; so you should keep thinking of what this course will mean to you until your desire is white hot. You should start this programme with an enthusiasm that will carry you through every session, triumphant to the end. Tell your friends that you have joined this course. Set aside one certain night of the week for the reading of these lessons and the preparation of your talks. In short, make it as easy as possible to go ahead. Make it as difficult as possible to retreat.

When Julius Caesar sailed over the channel from Gaul and landed with his legions on what is now England, what did he do to insure the success of his arms? A very clever thing: he halted his soldiers on the chalk cliffs of Dover, and, looking down over the waves two hundred feet below, they saw red tongues of fire consume every ship in which they had crossed. In the enemy's country, with the last link with the Continent gone, the last means of retreating burned, there was but one thing left for them to do: to advance, to conquer. That is precisely what they did.

Such was the spirit of the immortal Caesar. Why not make it yours, too, in this war to exterminate your foolish fear of audiences.

Second: Act Confidently

To develop courage when you are facing an audience, act as if you already have it. Of course, unless you are prepared, all the acting in the world will avail but little. But granted that you know what you are going to talk about, step out briskly and take a deep breath. In fact, breathe deeply for thirty seconds before you ever face your audience. The increased supply of oxygen will buoy you up and give you courage. The great tenor, Jean de Reszke, used to say that when you had your breath so you "could sit on it", nervousness vanished.

In every age, in every clime, men have always admired courage; so, no matter how your heart may be pounding inside, stride forth bravely, stop, stand still like the scourged youth of

Central Africa, and like him, act as if you loved it.

Draw yourself up to your full height and look your audience straight in the eyes, and begin to talk as confidently as if every one of them owed you money. Imagine that they do. Imagine that they have assembled there to bet you for an extension of credit. The psychological effect on you will be beneficial.

Do not nervously button and unbutton your coat, and fumble with your hands. If you must make nervous movements, place your hands behind your back and twist your fingers there where no one can see the performance—or wiggle your toes.

As a general rule, it is bad for a speaker to hide behind furniture, but it may give you a little courage the first few times to stand behind a table or chair and to grip them tightly—or hold a coin firmly in the palm of your hand.

So take the offensive against your fears. Go out to meet them, battle them, conquer them by sheer boldness at every opportunity.

Have a message, and then think of yourself as a courier boy instructed to deliver it. We pay slight attention to the boy. It is the courier that we want. The message—that is the thing. Keep your mind on it. Keep your heart in it. Know it like the back of your hand. Believe it feelingly. Then talk as if you were determined to say it. Do that, and the chances are ten to one that you will soon be master of the occasion and master of yourself.

Third: Know Thoroughly What You Are Going to Talk About

Unless a man has thought out and planned his talk and knows what he is going to say, he can't feel very comfortable when he faces his auditors. He is like the blind leading the blind. Under such circumstances, your speaker ought to be self-conscious, ought to feel repentant, ought to be ashamed of his negligence.

"I was elected to the Legislature in the autumn of 1881," Theodore Roosevelt wrote in his *Autobiography*, "and found myself the youngest man in that body. Like all young men and inexperienced members, I had considerable difficulty in teaching myself to speak. I profited much by the advice of a hard-headed old countryman—who was unconsciously paraphrasing the Duke of Wellington, who was himself doubtless paraphrasing somebody else. The advice ran: 'Don't speak until you are sure you have something to say, and know just what it is; then say it, and sit down.'"

This "hard-headed old countryman" ought to have told Roosevelt of another aid in overcoming nervousness. He ought to have added: "It will help you to throw off your embarrassment if you can find something to do before an audience—if you can exhibit something, write a word on the blackboard or point out a spot on the map, or move a table or throw open a window, or shift some books and papers—any physical action with a purpose behind it may help you to feel more at home."

True, it is not always easy to find an excuse for doing such things, but there is the suggestion. Use it if you can, but use it the first few times only. A baby does not cling to chairs after it learns to walk.

Fourth: Practice! Practice! Practice!

The last point we have to make here is emphatically the most important. Even though you forget everything you have read so far, do remember this: the first way, the last way, the never-failing way to develop self-confidence in speaking is—to speak. Really the whole matter finally simmers down to but one essential: practice, practice, practice. That is the *sine qua non* of it all, "the without which not".

"Any beginner," warned Roosevelt, "is apt to have 'buck fever'. 'Buck fever' means a state of intense nervous excitement which may be entirely divorced from timidity. It may affect a man the first time he has to speak to a large audience just as it may affect him the first time he sees a buck-deer or goes into battle. What such a man needs is not courage, but nerve control and cool-headedness. This he can get only by actual practice. He must, by custom and repeated exercise of self-mastery, get his nerves thoroughly under control. This is largely a matter of habit; in the sense of repeated effort and repeated exercise of willpower. If the man has the right stuff in him, he will grow stronger and stronger with each exercise of it."

So, persevere. Don't remain away from any session of the course because the business duties of the week have rendered it impossible for you to prepare something. Prepared or unprepared, come. Let the instructor, the class, suggest a topic for you after you have come before them.

You want to get rid of your audience fear? Let us see what causes it.

Fear is the result of a lack of confidence and what causes that? It is the result of not knowing what you can really do. And not knowing what you can do is caused by a lack of experience. When you get a record of successful experience behind you, your fears will vanish; they will melt like night mists under the glare of a July sun.

One thing is certain: the accepted way to learn to swim is to plunge into the water. You have been reading this book long enough. Let us toss it aside now, and get busy with the real work in hand.

Choose your subject, preferably one on which you have some knowledge, and construct a three-minute talk. Practice the talk by yourself a number of times. Then give it, if possible, to the group for whom it is intended, or before your class, putting into the effort all your force and power.

POINTS TO REMEMBER

1. The only way to win over fear of public speaking is by training and practicing.
2. Body language is important in order to appear confident.
3. Believe in the subject of your speech if you want the audience to believe it.

4

DO THIS AND YOU'LL BE WELCOME ANYWHERE

Why read this book to find out how to win friends? Why not study the technique of the greatest winner of friends the world has ever known? Who is he? You may meet him tomorrow coming down the street. When you get within ten feet of him, he will begin to wag his tail. If you stop and pat him, he will almost jump out of his skin to show you how much he likes you. And you know that behind this show of affection on his part, there are no ulterior motives: he doesn't want to sell you any real estate, and he doesn't want to marry you.

Did you ever stop to think that a dog is the only animal that doesn't have to work for a living? A hen has to lay eggs, a cow has to give milk, and a canary has to sing. But a dog makes his living by giving you nothing but love.

When I was five years old, my father bought a little yellow-haired pup for fifty cents. He was the light and joy of my childhood. Every afternoon about four-thirty, he would sit in the front yard with his beautiful eyes staring steadfastly at the path, and as soon as he heard my voice or saw me swinging my dinner pail through the buck brush, he was off like a shot, racing breathlessly up the hill to greet me with leaps of joy and barks of sheer ecstasy.

Tippy was my constant companion for five years. Then one tragic night—I shall never forget it—he was killed within ten feet of me, killed by lightning. Tippy's death was the tragedy of my boyhood.

You never read a book on psychology, Tippy. You didn't need to. You knew by some divine instinct that you can make more friends in two months by becoming genuinely interested in other people than you can in two years by trying to get other people interested in you. Let me repeat that. You can make more friends in two months by becoming interested in other people than you can in two years by trying to get other people interested in you.

Yet I know and you know people who blunder through life trying to wigwag other people into becoming interested in them.

Of course, it doesn't work. People are not interested in you. They are not interested in me. They are interested in themselves—morning, noon, and after dinner.

The New York Telephone Company made a detailed study of telephone conversations to find out which word is the most frequently used. You have guessed it: it is the personal pronoun "I." "I." "I." It was used 3,900 times in 500 telephone conversations. "I." "I." "I." "I."

When you see a group photograph that you are in, whose picture do you look for first?

If we merely try to impress people and get people interested in us, we will never have many true, sincere friends. Friends, real friends, are not made that way.

Napoleon tried it, and in his last meeting with Josephine he said: "Josephine, I have been as fortunate as any man ever was on this earth; and yet, at this hour, you are the only person in the world on whom I can rely." And historians doubt that he could rely even on her.

I spent an evening in the dressing room of Howard Thurston the last time he appeared on Broadway—Thurston was the acknowledged dean of magicians. For forty years he had traveled all over the world, time and again, creating illusions, mystifying audiences, and making people gasp with astonishment. More than 60 million people had paid admission to his show, and he had made almost $2 million in profit.

I asked Mr. Thurston to tell me the secret of his success. His schooling certainly had nothing to do with it, for he ran away from home as a small boy, became a hobo, rode in boxcars, slept in haystacks, begged his food from door to door, and learned to read by looking out of boxcars at signs along the railway.

Did he have a superior knowledge of magic? No, he told me hundreds of books had been written about legerdemain and scores of people knew as much about it as he did. But he had two things that the others didn't have. First, he had the ability to put his personality across the footlights. He was a master showman. He knew human nature. Everything he did, every gesture, every intonation of his voice, every lifting of an eyebrow had been carefully rehearsed, and his actions were timed to split seconds. But, in addition to that, Thurston had a genuine interest in people. He told me that many magicians would look at the audience and say to themselves, "Well, there is a bunch of suckers out there, a bunch of hicks; I'll fool them all right." But Thurston's method was totally different. He told me that every time he went on stage he said to himself: "I am grateful because these people came to see me. They make it possible for me to make my living in a very agreeable way. I'm going to give them the very best I possibly can."

I have discovered from personal experience that one can win the attention and time and cooperation of even the most sought-after people by becoming genuinely interested in them. Let me illustrate.

INVEST YOUR TIME AND ENERGY ON OTHERS

Years ago I conducted a course in fiction writing at the Brooklyn Institute of Arts and Sciences, and we wanted such distinguished and busy authors as Kathleen Norris, Fannie Hurst, Ida Tarbell, Albert Payson Terhune, and Rupert Hughes to come to Brooklyn and give us the benefit of their experience. So we wrote them, saying we admired their work and were deeply interested in getting their advice and learning the secrets of their success.

Each of these letters was signed by about 150 students. We said we realized that these authors were busy—too busy to prepare a lecture. So we enclosed a list of questions for them to answer about themselves and their methods of work. They liked that. Who wouldn't like it? So they left their homes and traveled to Brooklyn to give us a helping hand.

By using the same method, I persuaded Leslie M. Shaw, secretary of the treasury in Theodore Roosevelt's cabinet; George W. Wickersham, attorney general in Taft's cabinet; William Jennings Bryan; Franklin D. Roosevelt; and many other prominent men to come to talk to the students of my courses in public speaking.

All of us, be we workers in a factory, clerks in an office, or even a king upon his throne—all of us like people who admire us. Take the German kaiser, for example. At the close of World War I, he was probably the most savagely and universally despised man on this earth. Even his own nation turned against him when he fled over into Holland to save his neck. The hatred against him was so intense that millions of people would have loved to tear him limb from limb or burn him at the stake. In the midst of all this forest fire of fury, one little boy wrote the kaiser a simple, sincere letter glowing with kindliness and admiration. This little boy said that no matter what the others thought, he would always love Wilhelm as his emperor. The kaiser was deeply touched by his letter and invited the little boy to come see him. The boy came, so did his mother—and the kaiser married her. That little boy didn't need to read a book on how to win friends and influence people. He knew how instinctively.

If we want to make friends, let's put ourselves out to do things for other people—things that require time, energy, unselfishness, and thoughtfulness. When the Duke of Windsor was Prince of Wales, he was scheduled to tour South America, and before he started out on that tour he spent months studying Spanish so that he could make public talks in the language of the country; and the South Americans loved him for it.

For years I made it a point to find out the birthdays of my friends. How? Although I haven't the foggiest bit of faith in astrology, I began by asking the other party whether he believed the date of one's birth has anything to do with character and disposition. I then asked him or her to tell me the month and day of birth. If he or she said November 24, for example, I kept repeating to myself, "November 24, November 24." The minute my friend's back was turned, I wrote down the name and birthday and later would transfer it to a birthday book. At the beginning of each year, I had these birthday dates scheduled in my calendar pad so that they came to my attention automatically. When the natal day arrived, there was my letter or telegram. What a hit it made! I was frequently the only person on earth who remembered.

If we want to make friends, let's greet people with animation and enthusiasm. When somebody calls you on the telephone use the same psychology. Say "Hello" in tones that bespeak how pleased you are to have the person call. Many companies train their telephone operators to greet all callers in a tone that radiates interest and enthusiasm. The callers feel the company is concerned about them. Let's remember that when we answer the telephone tomorrow.

Showing a genuine interest in others not only wins friends for you, but may develop in its customers a loyalty to your company.

A show of interest, as with every other principle of human relations, must be sincere. It must pay off not only for the person showing the interest, but for the person receiving the attention. It is a two-way street—both parties benefit.

If you want others to like you, if you want to develop real friendships, if you want to help others at the same time as you help yourself, keep this principle in mind:

POINTS TO REMEMBER

1. The universal rule of "I."
2. One can win the attention and time and cooperation of even the most sought-after people by becoming genuinely interested in them.
3. The significance of relationships in your personal and professional world.

5

MAKE A GOOD FIRST IMPRESSION

At a dinner party in New York, one of the guests, a woman who had inherited money, was eager to make a pleasing impression on everyone. She had squandered a modest fortune on sables, diamonds and pearls. But she hadn't done anything whatever about her face. It radiated sourness and selfishness. She didn't realize what everyone knows: namely, that the expression one wears on one's face is far more important than the clothes one wears on one's back.

Charles Schwab told me his smile had been worth a million dollars. And he was probably understating the truth. For Schwab's personality, his charm, his ability to make people like him, were almost wholly responsible for his extraordinary success; and one of the most delightful factors in his personality was his captivating smile.

Actions speak louder than words, and a smile says, "I like you. You make me happy. I am glad to see you."

That is why dogs make such a hit. They are so glad to see us that they almost jump out of their skins. So, naturally, we are glad to see them.

A baby's smile has the same effect.

Have you ever been in a doctor's waiting room and looked around at all the glum faces waiting impatiently to be seen? Dr.

Stephen K. Sproul, a veterinarian in Raytown, Missouri, told of a typical spring day when his waiting room was full of clients waiting to have their pets inoculated. No one was talking to anyone else, and all were probably thinking of a dozen other things they would rather be doing than "wasting time" sitting in that office. He told one of our classes: There were six or seven clients waiting when a young woman came in with a nine-months-old baby and a kitten. As luck would have it, she sat down next to a gentleman who was more than a little distraught about the long wait for service. The next thing he knew, the baby just looked up at him with that great big smile that is so characteristic of babies. What did that gentleman do? Just what you and I would do, of course; he smiled back at the baby. Soon he struck up a conversation with the woman about her baby and his grandchildren, and soon the entire reception room joined in, and the boredom and tension were converted into a pleasant and enjoyable experience.

An insincere grin? No. That doesn't fool anybody. We know it is mechanical and we resent it. I am talking about a real smile, a heartwarming smile, a smile that comes from within, the kind of smile that will bring a good price in the marketplace.

Professor James V. McConnell, a psychologist at the University of Michigan, expressed his feelings about a smile. "People who smile," he said, "tend to manage, teach and sell more effectively, and to raise happier children. There's far more information in a smile than a frown. That's why encouragement is a much more effective teaching device than punishment."

The employment manager of a large New York department store told me she would rather hire a sales clerk who hadn't finished grade school, if he or she has a pleasant smile, than to hire a doctor of philosophy with a sombre face.

The effect of a smile is powerful—even when it is unseen.

Telephone companies throughout the United States have a programme called "phone power" which is offered to employees who use the telephone for selling their services or products. In this programme they suggest that you smile when talking on the phone. Your "smile" comes through in your voice.

THE MAGIC SMILE

The chairman of the board of directors of one of the largest rubber companies in the United States told me that, according to his observations, people rarely succeed at anything unless they have fun doing it. This industrial leader doesn't put much faith in the old adage that hard work alone is the magic key that will unlock the door to our desires. "I have known people," he said, "who succeeded because they had a rip-roaring good time conducting their business. Later, I saw those people change as the fun became work. The business had grown dull. They lost all joy in it, and they failed."

You must have a good time meeting people if you expect them to have a good time meeting you.

You don't feel like smiling? Then what? Two things. First, force yourself to smile. If you are alone, force yourself to whistle or hum a tune or sing. Act as if you were already happy, and that will tend to make you happy. Here is the way the psychologist and philosopher William James put it:

"Action seems to follow feeling, but really action and feeling go together; and by regulating the action, which is under the more direct control of the will, we can indirectly regulate the feeling, which is not.

"Thus the sovereign voluntary path to cheerfulness, if our cheerfulness be lost, is to sit up cheerfully and to act and speak as if cheerfulness were already there..."

Everybody in the world is seeking happiness—and there is one sure way to find it. That is by controlling your thoughts. Happiness doesn't depend on outward conditions. It depends on inner conditions.

It isn't what you have or who you are or where you are or what you are doing that makes you happy or unhappy. It is what you think about it. For example, two people may be in the same place, doing the same thing; both may have about an equal amount of money and prestige—and yet one may be miserable and the other happy. Why? Because of a different mental attitude. I have seen just as many happy faces among the poor peasants toiling with their primitive tools in the devastating heat of the tropics as I have seen in air-conditioned offices in New York, Chicago or Los Angeles.

"There is nothing either good or bad," said Shakespeare, "but thinking makes it so."

Abe Lincoln once remarked that "most folks are about as happy as they make up their minds to be." He was right. I saw a vivid illustration of that truth as I was walking up the stairs of the Long Island Railroad station in New York. Directly in front of me thirty or forty crippled boys on canes and crutches were struggling up the stairs. One boy had to be carried up. I was astonished at their laughter and gaiety. I spoke about it to one of the men in charge of the boys. "Oh, yes," he said, "when a boy realizes that he is going to be a cripple for life, he is shocked at first; but after he gets over the shock, he usually resigns himself to his fate and then becomes as happy as normal boys."

I felt like taking my hat off to those boys. They taught me a lesson I hope I shall never forget.

POINTS TO REMEMBER

1. Smile, it doesn't charge you anything.
2. If you think about negative things only, you'll live a miserable life.
3. Your mental attitude determines your success.

6

EXPRESSING GENUINE INTEREST IN OTHERS

Expressing genuine interest in others—there's no better way to make people interested in you. People respond to people who are sincerely interested in them. They can't help but respond.

This is one of the most basic facts of human psychology. We are flattered by other people's attention. It makes us feel special. It makes us feel important. We want to be around people who show interest in us. We want to keep them close. We tend to reciprocate their interest by showing interest in them.

There are many different ways of doing so. An expression of interest can be as simple as using a pleasant voice on the telephone. When someone calls, say hello in a tone that implies, "I'm happy to hear from you." When you see a familiar face at the shopping mall, greet the person and express a genuine pleasure at the coincidence.

Smile at people. Learn their names and how to pronounce them. Get the spellings and the titles right. Remember their birthdays. Ask about their husbands and wives and children. "I always knew that Clarence Michalis was at Bristol-Myers," says David S. Taylor, secretary-treasurer of H.G. Wellington &

Company, Inc., an investment-brokerage firm. "The minute we met, that would click. I remember those two things together. Not everybody does. I have a memory bank that would connect people with businesses."

You never know when these names will come in handy. Taylor learned this lesson when he was working as an executive in the beverage industry. "When I worked for Canada Dry," he said, "it may be hard to think why, but it was important for me to know people in the airline industry. They were a big customer. Grumman Aircraft fed a lot of people, and they had a lot of vending machines that dispensed drinks.

"It was just an entree. You could call up and say, 'Look, I'm having a problem with such-and-such.' Remembering these names and having those connections was enormously helpful."

Taylor used this technique as the basis for forming genuine relationships with people. By taking the time to remember people's names and associations, he has been able to help bring people together and solve their problems.

Don't limit those expressions of interest to the so-called important people in your life. Chances are they already get plenty of attention. Don't forget the secretaries, the assistants, the receptionists, the messengers, and all the other underrecognized people who keep your life on track. Ask about their days. It's the right thing to do—and you'll be surprised how much quicker the mail arrives at your desk in the morning.

Don't make the same mistake. When you care about someone—a friend, a spouse, a colleague—by all means let that person know. And do it while you have the chance.

Even more important than expressing interest is showing it. Harrison Conference Services, Inc., is in the business of organizing meetings and seminars, worrying about all the logistics so the clients can keep their minds focused on the real work at hand. To thrive, a company like Harrison must show its guests, over and over again, that the staff is genuinely—almost singlemindedly—interested in them.

It's not enough to have beautiful conference facilities, as Harrison certainly does. It's not enough to have attractive rooms, first-rate cuisine, high-tech audiovisual equipment, or a plethora of recreational choices, all of which Harrison has. Unless the guests feel they're being treated with genuine interest and respect, they'll take their business elsewhere.

Once you start this process, it will quickly become a natural part of your life. Before you know it, you'll be expressing interest, showing interest, and really becoming more interested in the people around you. The added benefit is that a genuine interest in others will take you outside yourself and make you less focused on whatever your own problems are.

The more you stay focused on other people, the more rewarding your personal relationships will be and the fewer negative thoughts you will have. Not a bad payback for a few kind words.

An open, friendly, interested greeting is just as important when you're the new person in the office or the new business-owner in town. The message should not be, I'm here, now what can you do for me? It should be instead, I'm here, now what can I do for you?

So volunteer at the local hospital. Sign up as a Little League coach. Join the PTA. Get involved in a local charity. These are all ways of showing interest in the community, of saying, "I care about this place." Any one of these will help you meet new people in a comfortable environment. It will be fun. It will make you feel good about yourself. It will help you develop new relationships, gain self-confidence, and it will bring you out of your comfort zone.

THERE'S NOTHING MORE EFFECTIVE AND REWARDING THAN SHOWING A GENUINE INTEREST IN OTHER PEOPLE.

POINTS TO REMEMBER

1. The quickest way to make people interested in you is by showing your interest in them.
2. Make the effort to learn the name of the person you are interacting with; such small gestures go a long way.
3. Be a good listener to be an even better speaker.

7

LISTENING TO LEARN

There are two very good reasons to listen to other people. You learn things that way, and people respond to those who listen to them.

This point sounds so obvious it looks almost silly sitting there in cold, hard type. But it's a lesson that most of us spend most of our lives forgetting to apply.

Hugh Downs was lucky. The longtime host of ABC's *20/20* program found out about listening early in his broadcasting career. This was back in the days of radio, when Downs was just getting started as an on-air interviewer. He witnessed firsthand how a simple failure to listen could trip up one of his most experienced colleagues.

"He was interviewing a man who had escaped from a Kremlin prison in the thirties," Downs recalled. "This guest was telling him how, for months, the prisoners had been trying to tunnel their way out of there. They'd dug and dug. They'd eaten the dirt. They'd arranged to have a saw smuggled in. And when they figured their tunnel was outside the prison walls, they began digging up. It was quite a dramatic story.

"Then this one midnight, they were finally ready to break loose. They had already sawed through a wooden platform above their heads. But when this one prisoner stuck his head out, he was shocked by what he saw. 'When I got up,' he told the interviewer, 'I realized I was right in the middle of Josef Stalin's office.'

"And do you know what this interviewer said next?" Downs asked, recalling that long-ago day. "'Do you have any hobbies?'"

Not "Are you serious? Josef Stalin's office?" Or "Stalin wasn't working late that night, I hope." Or "So tell me, were you tempted to plop down in the butcher's chair and light up one of his cigars?" Had the interviewer been listening at all, he would have known to ask any number of follow-up questions the members of his audience undoubtedly had on their minds. But the interviewer's attention was off somewhere else. All he could manage was that ridiculous non sequitur. And his listeners were deprived of the climax to a fascinating tale.

"That's a true story," Downs said. "And I've heard other interviews like that, where the interviewer just didn't listen. It's amazing what people can miss. It's a part of the business I call the yeah-well interview."

The importance of listening doesn't apply just to professional interviewers, of course. It is vital for anyone, anywhere, anytime, who hopes to communicate with others.

Listening is the single most important of all the communication skills. More important than stirring oratory. More important than a powerful voice. More important than the ability to speak multiple languages. More important even than a flair for the written word.

Good listening is truly where effective communication begins. It's surprising how few people really listen well, but successful leaders, more often than not, are the ones who have learned the value of listening.

"I don't sit on top of a mountain and get these visions of what we ought to do," says Richard C. Buetow, director of quality at Motorola, Inc. "I have to find out from other people. I have to do a lot of listening."

Even a great communicator like Buetow, who is expected to articulate and communicate the Motorola vision just about everywhere he goes, must also know when not to talk. In his words, "You have to be able to turn off your transmitter and listen—put the receiver on, let other people articulate ideas, and nurture them."

This understanding is a central part of Buetow's self-image as a business leader. He never talks about himself, for instance, as a grand strategist or a sophisticated corporate sage. He compares himself instead to a carrier pigeon.

"I don't solve one quality problem at Motorola," he explains. "If you ask me to do hardware, first thing I'll do is give you the telephone number of the person who is responsible for hardware. What I do is take the good ideas that I hear and carry them from place to place."

The underlying truth here is self-evident: *No one can possibly know everything. Listening to others is the single best way to learn.*

This means listening to employees, to customers, and to your friends and family—even to what harshest critics have to say. It doesn't mean becoming a captive of other people's opinions, but it does mean hearing them out.

You'll be thankful for many of their ideas.

Giorgio Maschietto, managing director of Lever Chile, S.A., the packaged-goods company, was responsible for running a string of factories in South America, including a giant Pepsodent toothpaste plant. The factory's production schedule was constantly being interrupted by the need to wash out the steel toothpaste tanks. One day one of the line operators made a suggestion, and Maschietto had the good sense to follow through.

"We were using just one tank," he recalls. "This line employee suggested we should put in a second tank. Now we can wash the first tank while using the second one, so there's no need to stop production anymore for tank washing. By adding a bolt in one case and by adding a small tank in another case, we've reduced changeover time by seventy percent and significantly increased productivity."

From the same source—the factory floor—Maschietto got a second toothpaste-production idea that was just as important. For years the factory had used a set of highly delicate and highly expensive scales beneath the toothpaste conveyer belt. Their purpose was to make sure each carton of toothpaste actually contained a tube. But the high-tech scales never quite worked. "Sometimes," Maschietto says, "we used to seal up empty cartons and send them out.

"One of the ideas of the men on the line was to replace all this expensive machinery and just put a small jet of air across the conveyer belt where the tubes rolled by. The compressed air is regulated so that when the carton is empty, the pressure of the air is enough to throw the empty cartons off the belt."

BE AN ACTIVE PARTICIPANT IN CONVERSATIONS

Many people think of listening as passive, talking as active. Even the clichés people use in conversation—"sit back and listen"—hint at this pervasive misunderstanding of what true listening is about. Simply hearing what someone says is a relatively passive activity. But engaged, effective listening is a highly active sport.

Andrés Navarro, president of SONDA, S.A., a South American computer-systems company, uses his native Spanish language to illustrate the difference between the two. "In Spanish," Navarro explains, "we have two words, *oir* and *escuchar*," the rough equivalent of "to hear" and "to listen." "To really listen is much more than just hearing. Many people, when they are hearing someone, they are really thinking to themselves, 'What will I answer?' instead of trying to listen to what the person is saying."

Active listening requires an intense involvement in a conversation, even when the listener's lips are still. That isn't always easy. It takes concentration. It requires genuine engagement. It calls for questioning and prodding. And it demands some kind of response, quick, thoughtful, on target, and concise.

There are many ways of displaying active involvement in a conversation, ways that don't entail jumping in and interrupting the other person's every seven words. The trick isn't to master every one of these techniques. Good listeners learn a few that they find comfortable and natural—and remember to put these few to work.

It can be an occasional nod, or an uh-huh, or an I see. Some people like to shift their postures or lean forward in the chair. At appropriate moments, others smile or shake their heads. Strong eye contact is another way of indicating to your conversation-mate, "Yes, I am listening closely to what you are telling me."

And when the other person comes to a break in his or her talking, go ahead and ask a question that follows closely from what was just said.

What's important here isn't the precise listening technique that is chosen. None of these methods should ever be used in a wooden or rote way. These are just a few approaches that are worth being mindful of when the moment feels right. They will make the other person happier about speaking with you.

Elmer Wheeler was driving at much the same idea two

generations ago when he wrote in his seminal book on salesmanship, *Sell the Sizzle Not the Steak*, "A good listener bends toward you physically. He leans on you mentally with every word that you utter. He is 'with you' every moment, nodding and smiling at the right times. He listens 'a little closer'." This isn't good advice just for salesmen, Wheeler wrote. "It is a sound rule to follow for social and business success."

"A person who's actively listening," says Bill Makahilahila, Director of Human Resources at SGS-Thomson Microelectronics, Inc., "is usually the one who is asking questions and then waiting for a response, as opposed to coming up with an instant solution. Active listening is occurring when the employee feels and knows beyond a shadow of a doubt that you're not just jumping to conclusions."

Makahilahila thinks this is such an important concept that he has even created an Active Listening Award for SGS-Thomson supervisors who excel at listening. He has come up with a three-question test for determining whether someone is listening actively or not:

1. Do you ask questions and wait for an answer?
2. Do you respond quickly and directly to the questions that are asked?
3. Does the other person *feel* you are listening actively to him or her?

A good listening environment—that's where listening begins. It's impossible to ever listen effectively when fear, anxiety, or nervousness is present. That's why good teachers always make sure their classrooms are comfortable, hospitable places.

"I know for myself that when I'm nervous about something, I don't listen as well," says kindergarten teacher Barbara Hammerman. "I'm concerned with my own being. If the children are tense and nervous in a classroom, they're not free to listen."

William Savel, retired chairman of Baskin-Robbins, the worldwide ice-cream and yogurt retailer, was once sent to Japan by the Nestlé Company to run marketing and sales.

"The first thing I did was to visit with a number of U.S. companies that had Japanese subsidiaries," he recalls. He learned to speak Japanese. He slept in Japanese hotels. He ate Japanese food. He did everything he could think of to surround himself with things Japanese.

"The important thing is to listen," Savel said, "to really listen before you go in and start shooting your mouth off and telling everybody how smart you are. You've got to learn how dumb you are first. You have to go in and get to know the people, interact with them, don't put yourself above anyone else. Get around, talk to everybody, listen very intently, and don't make up your mind too fast."

Simply put, *People everywhere love to be listened to, and they almost always respond to others who listen to them.* Listening is one of the best techniques we have for showing respect to someone else. It's an indication that we consider them important human beings. It's our way of saying, "What you think and do and believe is important to me."

Strangely enough, listening to someone else's opinions is often the best method of getting them around to your way of thinking. Dean Rusk, President Johnson's secretary of state, knew this from decades of negotiating with some of the world's most stubborn political leaders. "Listening is the way to persuade others with your ears." It's true; listening can be a tremendously powerful tool for convincing others to see the world the way that you do.

"The real key," says merchant banker Tom Saunders, of

Saunders Karp & Company, "is getting to understand a person and what he values and how he wants to look at investments and whether or not you could honestly say our approach was right and compatible for him."

Saunders is in the business of advising big corporations about how to invest prodigious sums of money. His number-one technique? Listening to them. It all "goes back to listening," he says. "What was really on his mind? Why had he said no? What was the real reason behind it?

"I've had a twenty-five-year relationship with AT&T, which has just been extraordinary. I think it's all basically been due to listening."

Saunders goes on, "I can give you the best-looking brochure. I can throw up all these slides. But still I've got to find out what's in there that's interesting to that person. What's on this person's mind? What does he think about? How does he look at things?"

The first step to becoming a strong, active listener is understanding how important good listening is. The second step is wanting to learn. Finally, you have to practice those budding listening skills.

"I learned mine in not such a pleasant way," recalls Wolfgang R. Schmitt, chief executive officer of Rubbermaid, Incorporated, the home-products giant. "I learned mine by going through a divorce when I was young. I was very career-centered. In the process of trying to avoid the divorce, we went to a counselor. That was really the first time I understood how crucial good listening is. Here was something that was important to me—my marriage—and I wanted to try to retrieve it. That was the first time that somebody said to me some very straightforward things."

About listening? "Not just listening," Schmitt says, "but

internalizing other people's feelings and thinking about them. Then being able to mirror them back, so you can demonstrate their importance to you."

The simple truth of the matter is that people love being listened to. It's true in the business world. It's true at home. It's true of just about everyone we come across in life.

"The secret of influencing people lies not so much in being a good talker as in being a good listener," Dale Carnegie wrote. "Most people trying to win others to their way of thinking do too much talking themselves. Let the other people talk themselves out. They know more about their business or problems than you do. So ask them questions. Let them tell you a few things.

"If you disagree with them, you may be tempted to interrupt. But don't. It's dangerous. They won't pay attention to you while they still have a lot of ideas of theirs crying for expression. So listen patiently and with an open mind. Be sincere about it. Encourage them to express their ideas fully."

They will never forget. And you will learn a thing or two.

NOBODY IS MORE PERSUASIVE THAN A GOOD LISTENER.

POINTS TO REMEMBER

1. Effective communication begins with good listening.
2. Everyone wants to be heard.
3. You can influence people to go along with your ideas by conversing with them.

8

THE TRUTH ABOUT GESTURE

Gesture is really a simple matter that requires observation and common sense rather than a book of rules. Gesture is an outward expression of an inward condition. It is merely an effect—the effect of a mental or an emotional impulse struggling for expression through physical avenues.

You must not, however, begin at the wrong end: if you are troubled by your gestures, or a lack of gestures, attend to the cause, not the effect. It will not in the least help matters to tack on to your delivery a few mechanical movements. If the tree in your front yard is not growing to suit you, fertilize and water the soil and let the tree have sunshine. Obviously it will not help your tree to nail on a few branches. If your cistern is dry, wait until it rains; or bore a well. Why plunge a pump into a dry hole?

The speaker whose thoughts and emotions are welling within him like a mountain spring will not have much trouble to make gestures; it will be merely a question of properly directing them. If his enthusiasm for his subject is not such as to give him a natural impulse for dramatic action, it will avail nothing to furnish him with a long list of rules. He may tack on some movements, but they will look like the wilted branches nailed to a tree to simulate life. Gestures must be born, not built. A wooden horse may amuse the children, but it takes a live one to go somewhere.

It is not only impossible to lay down definite rules on this subject, but it would be silly to try, for everything depends on the speech, the occasion, the personality and feelings of the speaker, and the attitude of the audience. It is easy enough to forecast the result of multiplying seven by six, but it is impossible to tell any man what kind of gestures he will be impelled to use when he wishes to show his earnestness. We may tell him that many speakers close the hand, with the exception of the forefinger, and pointing that finger straight at the audience pour out their thoughts like a volley; or that others stamp one foot for emphasis; or that Mr. Bryan often slaps his hands together for great force, holding one palm upward in an easy manner; or that Gladstone would sometimes make a rush at the clerk's table in Parliament and smite it with his hand so forcefully that Disraeli once brought down the house by grimly congratulating himself that such a barrier stood between himself and "the honorable gentleman."

All these things, and a bookful more, may we tell the speaker, but we cannot know whether he can use these gestures or not, any more than we can decide whether he could wear Mr. Bryan's clothes. The best that can be done on this subject is to offer a few practical suggestions, and let personal good taste decide as to where effective dramatic action ends and extravagant motion begins.

ANY GESTURE THAT MERELY CALLS ATTENTION TO ITSELF IS BAD

The purpose of a gesture is to carry your thought and feeling into the minds and hearts of your hearers; this it does by emphasizing your message, by interpreting it, by expressing it in action, by striking its tone in either a physically descriptive, a suggestive, or a typical gesture—and let it be remembered all the time that gesture includes all physical movement, from facial expression and the tossing of the head to the expressive movements of hand and foot. A shifting of the pose may be a most effective gesture.

What is true of gesture is true of all life. If the people on the street turn around and watch your walk, your walk is more important than you are—change it. If the attention of your audience is called to your gestures, they are not convincing, because they appear to be—what they have a doubtful right to be in reality—studied. Have you ever seen a speaker use such grotesque gesticulations that you were fascinated by their frenzy of oddity, but could not follow his thought? Do not smother ideas with gymnastics. Savonarola would rush down from the high pulpit among the congregation in the duomo at Florence and carry the fire of conviction to his hearers; Billy Sunday slides to base on the platform carpet in dramatizing one of his baseball illustrations. Yet in both instances the message has somehow stood out bigger than the gesture—it is chiefly in calm afterthought that men have remembered the form of dramatic expression. When Sir Henry Irving made his famous exit as Shylock, the last thing the audience saw was his pallid, avaricious hand extended skinny and claw-like against the background. At the time, every one was overwhelmed by the tremendous typical quality of this gesture; now, we have time to think of its art, and discuss its realistic power.

Only when gesture is subordinated to the absorbing importance of the idea—a spontaneous, living expression of living truth—is it justifiable at all; and when it is remembered for itself—as a piece of unusual physical energy or as a poem of grace—it is a dead failure as dramatic expression. There is a place for a unique style of walking—it is the circus or the cake-walk; there is a place for surprisingly rhythmical evolutions of arms and legs—it is on the dance floor or the stage. Don't let your agility and grace put your thoughts out of business.

One of the present writers took his first lesson in gesture from a certain college president who knew far more about what had happened at the Diet of Worms than he did about how to express himself in action. His instructions were to start the movement on a certain word, continue it on a precise curve, and unfold the fingers at the conclusion, ending with the forefinger—just so. Plenty, and more than plenty, has been published on this subject, giving just such silly directions. Gesture is a thing of mentality and feeling—not a matter of geometry. Remember, whenever a pair of shoes, a method of pronunciation, or a gesture calls attention to itself, it is bad. When you have made really good gestures in a good speech your hearers will not go away saying, "What beautiful gestures he made!" but they will say, "I'll vote for that measure." "He is right—I believe in that."

GESTURES SHOULD BE BORN OF THE MOMENT

The best actors and public speakers rarely know in advance what gestures they are going to make. They make one gesture on certain words tonight, and none at all tomorrow night at the same point—their various moods and interpretations govern their gestures. It is all a matter of impulse and intelligent feeling with them—don't overlook that word intelligent. Nature does not always provide the same kind of sunsets or snow flakes, and the movements of a good speaker vary almost as much as the creations of nature.

Now all this is not to say that you must not take some thought for your gestures. If that were meant, why this chapter? When the sergeant despairingly besought the recruit in the awkward squad to step out and look at himself, he gave splendid advice—and worthy of personal application. Particularly while you are in the learning days of public speaking you must learn to criticize your own gestures. Recall them—see where they were useless, crude, awkward, what not, and do better next time. There is a vast deal of difference between being conscious of self and being self-conscious.

It will require your nice discrimination in order to cultivate spontaneous gestures and yet give due attention to practice. While you depend upon the moment it is vital to remember that only a dramatic genius can effectively accomplish such feats as we have related of Whitefield, Savonarola, and others: and doubtless the first time they were used they came in a burst of spontaneous feeling, yet Whitefield declared that not until he had delivered a sermon forty times was its delivery perfected. What spontaneity initiates, let practice complete. Every effective speaker and every vivid actor has observed, considered and practiced gesture until his dramatic actions are a sub-conscious possession, just like his ability to pronounce correctly without especially concentrating his thought. Every able platform man has possessed himself of a dozen ways in which he might depict in gesture any given emotion; in fact, the means for such expression are endless—and this is precisely why it is both useless and harmful to make a chart of gestures and enforce them as the ideals of what may be used to express this or that feeling. Practice descriptive, suggestive, and typical movements until they come as naturally as a good articulation; and rarely forecast the gestures you will use at a given moment: leave something to that moment.

AVOID MONOTONY IN GESTURE

Roast beef is an excellent dish, but it would be terrible as an exclusive diet. No matter how effective one gesture is, do not overwork it. Put variety in your actions. Monotony will destroy all beauty and power. The pump handle makes one effective gesture, and on hot days that one is very eloquent, but it has its limitations.

ANY MOVEMENT THAT IS NOT SIGNIFICANT, WEAKENS

Do not forget that. Restlessness is not expression. A great many useless movements will only take the attention of the audience from what you are saying. A widely-noted man introduced the speaker of the evening one Sunday lately to a New York audience. The only thing remembered about that introductory speech is that the speaker played nervously with the covering of the table as he talked. We naturally watch moving objects. A janitor putting down a window can take the attention of the hearers from Mr. Roosevelt. By making a few movements at one side of the stage a chorus girl may draw the interest of the spectators from a big scene between the 'leads.' When our forefathers lived in caves they had to watch moving objects, for movements meant danger. We have not yet overcome the habit. Advertisers have taken advantage of it—witness the moving electric light signs in any city. A shrewd speaker will respect this law and conserve the attention of his audience by eliminating all unnecessary movements.

GESTURE SHOULD EITHER BE SIMULTANEOUS WITH OR PRECEDE THE WORDS—NOT FOLLOW THEM

Lady Macbeth says: "Bear welcome in your eye, your hand, your tongue." Reverse this order and you get comedy. Say, "There he goes," pointing at him after you have finished your words, and see if the result is not comical.

DO NOT MAKE SHORT, JERKY MOVEMENTS

Some speakers seem to be imitating a waiter who has failed to get a tip. Let your movements be easy, and from the shoulder, as a rule, rather than from the elbow. But do not go to the other extreme and make too many flowing motions—that savors of the lackadaisical.

Put a little "punch" and life into your gestures. You can not, however, do this mechanically. The audience will detect it if you do. They may not know just what is wrong, but the gesture will have a false appearance to them.

FACIAL EXPRESSION IS IMPORTANT

Have you ever stopped in front of a Broadway theater and looked at the photographs of the cast? Notice the row of chorus girls who are supposed to be expressing fear. Their attitudes are so mechanical that the attempt is ridiculous. Notice the picture of the 'star' expressing the same emotion: his muscles are drawn, his eyebrows lifted, he shrinks, and fear shines through his eyes. That actor felt fear when the photograph was taken. The chorus girls felt that it was time for a rarebit, and more nearly expressed that emotion than they did fear. Incidentally, that is one reason why they stay in the chorus.

The movements of the facial muscles may mean a great deal more than the movements of the hand. The man who sits in a dejected heap with a look of despair on his face is expressing his thoughts and feelings just as effectively as the man who is waving his arms and shouting from the back of a dray wagon. The eye has been called the window of the soul. Through it shines the light of our thoughts and feelings.

DO NOT USE TOO MUCH GESTURE

As a matter of fact, in the big crises of life we do not go through many actions. When your closest friend dies you do not throw up your hands and talk about your grief. You are more likely to sit and brood in dry-eyed silence. The Hudson River does not make much noise on its way to the sea—it is not half so loud as the little creek up in Bronx Park that a bullfrog could leap across. The barking dog never tears your trousers—at least they say he doesn't. Do not fear the man who waves his arms and shouts his anger, but the man who comes up quietly with eyes flaming and face burning may knock you down. Fuss is not force. Observe these principles in nature and practice them in your delivery.

The writer of this chapter once observed an instructor drilling a class in gesture. They had come to the passage from Henry VIII in which the humbled Cardinal says: "Farewell, a long farewell to all my greatness." It is one of the pathetic passages of literature. A man uttering such a sentiment would be crushed, and the last thing on earth he would do would be to make flamboyant movements. Yet this class had an elocutionary manual before them that gave an appropriate gesture for every occasion, from paying the gas bill to death-bed farewells. So they were instructed to throw their arms out at full length on each side and say: "Farewell, a long farewell to all my greatness." Such a gesture might possibly be used in an after-dinner speech at the convention of a telephone company whose lines extended from the Atlantic to the Pacific, but to think of Wolsey's using that movement would suggest that his fate was just.

POSTURE

The physical attitude to be taken before the audience really is included in gesture. Just what that attitude should be depends, not on rules, but on the spirit of the speech and the occasion. Senator La Follette stood for three hours with his weight thrown on his forward foot as he leaned out over the footlights, ran his fingers through his hair, and flamed out a denunciation of the trusts. It was very effective. But imagine a speaker taking that kind of position to discourse on the development of road-making machinery. If you have a fiery, aggressive message, and will let yourself go, nature will naturally pull your weight to your forward foot. A man in a hot political argument or a street brawl never has to stop to think upon which foot he should throw his weight. You may sometimes place your weight on your back foot if you have a restful and calm message—but don't worry about it: just stand like a man who genuinely feels what he is saying. Do not stand with your heels close together, like a soldier or a butler. No more should you stand with them wide apart like a traffic policeman. Use simple good manners and common sense.

Here a word of caution is needed. We have advised you to allow your gestures and postures to be spontaneous and not woodenly prepared beforehand, but do not go to the extreme of ignoring the importance of acquiring mastery of your physical movements. A muscular hand made flexible by free movement, is far more likely to be an effective instrument in gesture than a stiff, pudgy bunch of fingers. If your shoulders are lithe and carried well, while your chest does not retreat from association with your chin, the chances of using good extemporaneous gestures are so much the better. Learn to keep the back of your neck touching your collar, hold your chest high, and keep down your waist measure.

So attention to strength, poise, flexibility, and grace of body are the foundations of good gesture, for they are expressions of vitality, and without vitality no speaker can enter the kingdom of power. When an awkward giant like Abraham Lincoln rose to the sublimest heights of oratory he did so because of the greatness of his soul—his very ruggedness of spirit and artless honesty were properly expressed in his gnarly body. The fire of character, of earnestness, and of message swept his hearers before him when the tepid words of an insincere Apollo would have left no effect. But be sure you are a second Lincoln before you despise the handicap of physical awkwardness.

"Ty" Cobb has confided to the public that when he is in a batting slump he even stands before a mirror, bat in hand, to observe the "swing" and "follow through" of his batting form. If you would learn to stand well before an audience, look at yourself in a mirror—but not too often. Practice walking and standing before the mirror so as to conquer awkwardness—not to cultivate a pose. Stand on the platform in the same easy manner that you would use before guests in a drawing-room. If your position is not graceful, make it so by dancing, gymnasium work, and by getting grace and poise in your mind.

Do not continually hold the same position. Any big change of thought necessitates a change of position. Be at home. There are no rules—it is all a matter of taste. While on the platform forget that you have any hands until you desire to use them—then remember them effectively. Gravity will take care of them. Of course, if you want to put them behind you, or fold them once in awhile, it is not going to ruin your speech. Thought and feeling are the big things in speaking—not the position of a foot or a hand. Simply put your limbs where you want them to be—you have a will, so do not neglect to use it.

Let us reiterate, do not despise practice. Your gestures and movements may be spontaneous and still be wrong. No matter how natural they are, it is possible to improve them.

It is impossible for anyone—even yourself—to criticize your gestures until after they are made. You can't prune a peach tree until it comes up; therefore speak much, and observe your own speech. While you are examining yourself, do not forget to study statuary and paintings to see how the great portrayers of nature have made their subjects express ideas through action. Notice the gestures of the best speakers and actors. Observe the physical expression of life everywhere. The leaves on the tree respond to the slightest breeze. The muscles of your face, the light of your eyes, should respond to the slightest change of feeling. Emerson says: "Every man that I meet is my superior in some way. In that I learn of him." Illiterate Italians make gestures so wonderful and beautiful that Booth or Barrett might have sat at their feet and been instructed. Open your eyes. Emerson says again: "We are immersed in beauty, but our eyes have no clear vision." Toss this book to one side; go out and watch one child plead with another for a bite of apple; see a street brawl; observe life in action. Do you want to know how to express victory? Watch the victors' hands go high on election night. Do you want to plead a cause? Make a composite photograph of all the pleaders in daily life you constantly see. Beg, borrow, and steal the best you can get, BUT DON'T

GIVE IT OUT AS THEFT. Assimilate it until it becomes a part of you—then let the expression come out.

POINTS TO REMEMBER

1. Good gestures aren't something you are inherently born with. They require work.
2. Restless movements appear unattractive.
3. Observe the gestures that famous speakers and actors make.

9

NO ONE LIKES TO TAKE ORDERS

I once had the pleasure of dining with Mrs. Ida Tarbell, the dean of American biographers. When I told her I was writing this book, we began discussing this all-important subject of getting along with people, and she told me that while she was writing her biography of Owen D. Young, she interviewed a man who had sat for three years in the same office with Mr. Young. This man declared that during all that time he had never heard Owen D. Young give a direct order to anyone. He always gave suggestions, not orders. Owen D. Young never said, for example, "Do this or do that," or "Don't do this or don't do that." He would say, "You might consider this," or "Do you think that would work?" Frequently he would say, after he had dictated a letter, "What do you think of this?" In looking over a letter of one of his assistants, he would say, "Maybe if we were to phrase it this way it would be better." He always gave people the opportunity to do things themselves; he never told his assistants to do things; he let them do them, let them learn from their mistakes.

A technique like that makes it easy for a person to correct errors. A technique like that saves a person's pride and gives him or her a feeling of importance. It encourages cooperation instead of rebellion.

Resentment caused by a brash order may last a long time—even if the order was given to correct an obviously bad situation. Dan Santarelli, a teacher at a vocational school in Wyoming, Pennsylvania, told one of our classes how one of his students had blocked the entranceway to one of the school's shops by illegally parking his car in it. One of the other instructors stormed into the classroom and asked in an arrogant tone, "Whose car is blocking the driveway?" When the student who owned the car responded, the instructor screamed: "Move that car and move it right now, or I'll wrap a chain around it and drag it out of there."

Now that student was wrong. The car should not have been parked there. But from that day on, not only did that student resent the instructor's action, but all the students in the class did everything they could to give the instructor a hard time and make his job unpleasant.

How could he have handled it differently? If he had asked in a friendly way, "Whose car is in the driveway?" and then suggested that if it were moved, other cars could get in and out, the student would have gladly moved it and neither he nor his classmates would have been upset and resentful.

Asking questions not only makes an order more palatable; it often stimulates the creativity of the persons whom you ask. People are more likely to accept an order if they have had a part in the decision that caused the order to be issued.

When Ian Macdonald of Johannesburg, South Africa, the general manager of a small manufacturing plant specializing in precision machine parts, had the opportunity to accept a very large order, he was convinced that he would not meet the promised delivery date. The work already scheduled in the shop and the short completion time needed for this order made it seem impossible for him to accept the order.

Instead of pushing his people to accelerate their work and rush the order through, he called everybody together, explained the situation to them, and told them how much it would mean to the company and to them if they could make it possible to produce the order on time. Then he started asking questions:

"Is there anything we can do to handle this order?"

"Can anyone think of different ways to process it through the shop that will make it possible to take the order?"

"Is there any way to adjust our hours or personnel assignments that would help?"

The employees came up with many ideas and insisted that he take the order. They approached it with a "We can do it" attitude, and the order was accepted, produced, and delivered on time.

POINTS TO REMEMBER

1. It is not necessary to directly call out someone on their mistake.
2. Leave the accusatory tone and opt for a friendly one.
3. Create a safe space for everyone around you so they can come to you with problems.

10

"IF YOU WANT TO GATHER HONEY, DON'T KICK OVER THE BEEHIVE"

Criticism is futile because it puts a person on the defensive and usually makes him strive to justify himself. Criticism is dangerous, because it wounds a person's precious pride, hurts his sense of importance, and arouses resentment.

B. F. Skinner, the world-famous psychologist, proved through his experiments that an animal rewarded for good behavior will learn much more rapidly and retain what it learns far more effectively than an animal punished for bad behavior. Later studies have shown that the same applies to humans. By criticizing, we do not make lasting changes and often incur resentment.

Hans Selye, another great psychologist, said, "As much as we thirst for approval, we dread condemnation."

The resentment that criticism engenders can demoralize employees, family members, and friends, and still not correct the situation that has been condemned.

George B. Johnston of Enid, Oklahoma, is the safety coordinator for an engineering company. One of his responsibilities is to see that employees wear their hard hats whenever they are on the job in the field. He reported that whenever he came across workers who were not wearing hard hats, he would tell them with a lot of authority of the regulation and that they must comply. As a result he would get sullen acceptance, and often after he left, the workers would remove the hats.

He decided to try a different approach. The next time he found some of the workers not wearing their hard hats, he asked if the hats were uncomfortable or did not fit properly. Then he reminded the men in a pleasant tone of voice that the hat was designed to protect them from injury and suggested that it always be worn on the job. The result was increased compliance with the regulation with no resentment or emotional upset.

You will find examples of the futility of criticism bristling on a thousand pages of history. Take, for example, the famous quarrel between Theodore Roosevelt and President Taft—a quarrel that split the Republican party, put Woodrow Wilson in the White House, and wrote bold, luminous lines across the First World War and altered the flow of history. Let's review the facts quickly. When Theodore Roosevelt stepped out of the White House in 1908, he supported Taft, who was elected president. Then Theodore Roosevelt went off to Africa to shoot lions. When he returned, he exploded. He denounced Taft for his conservatism, tried to secure the nomination for a third term himself, formed the Bull Moose party, and all but demolished the GOP. In the election that followed, William Howard Taft and the Republican party carried only two states, Vermont and Utah—the most disastrous defeat the party had ever known.

Theodore Roosevelt blamed Taft, but did President Taft blame himself? Of course not. With tears in his eyes, Taft said: "I don't see how I could have done any differently from what I have."

Who was to blame? Roosevelt or Taft? Frankly, I don't

know, and I don't care. The point I am trying to make is that all of Theodore Roosevelt's criticism didn't persuade Taft that he was wrong. It merely made Taft strive to justify himself and to reiterate with tears in his eyes: "I don't see how I could have done any differently from what I have."

There you are; human nature in action, wrongdoers, blaming everybody but themselves. We are all like that. So when you and I are tempted to criticize someone tomorrow, let's remember Al Capone, "Two Gun" Crowley, and Albert Fall. Let's realize that criticisms are like homing pigeons. They always return home. Let's realize that the person we are going to correct and condemn will probably justify himself or herself, and condemn us in return; or, like the gentle Taft, will say: "I don't see how I could have done any differently from what I have."

COMPLY BY LINCOLN'S LIFE CODES

On the morning of April 15, 1865, Abraham Lincoln lay dying in a hall bedroom of a cheap lodging house directly across the street from Ford's Theater, where John Wilkes Booth had shot him. Lincoln's long body lay stretched diagonally across a sagging bed that was too short for him. A cheap reproduction of Rosa Bonheur's famous painting *The Horse Fair* hung above the bed, and a dismal gas jet flickered yellow light.

As Lincoln lay dying, Secretary of War Stanton said, "There lies the most perfect ruler of men that the world has ever seen."

What was the secret of Lincoln's success in dealing with people? I studied the life of Abraham Lincoln for ten years and devoted all of three years to writing and rewriting a book entitled *Lincoln the Unknown.* I believe I have made as detailed and exhaustive a study of Lincoln's personality and home life as it is possible for any being to make. I made a special study of Lincoln's method of dealing with people. Did he indulge in criticism? Oh, yes. As a young man in the Pigeon Creek Valley of Indiana, he not only criticized but also wrote letters and poems ridiculing people and dropped these letters on the country roads where they were sure to be found. One of these letters aroused resentments that burned for a lifetime.

Even after Lincoln had become a practicing lawyer in Springfield, Illinois, he attacked his opponents openly in letters published in the newspapers. But he did this just once too often.

In the autumn of 1842 he ridiculed a vain, pugnacious politician by the name of James Shields. Lincoln lampooned him through an anonymous letter published in the Springfield *Journal.* The town roared with laughter. Shields, sensitive and proud, boiled with indignation. He found out who wrote the letter, leaped on his horse, started after Lincoln, and challenged him to fight a duel. Lincoln didn't want to fight. He was opposed to dueling, but he couldn't get out of it and save his honor. He was given the choice of weapons. Since he had very long arms, he chose cavalry broadswords and took lessons in sword fighting from a West Point graduate. On the appointed day, he and Shields met on a sandbar in the Mississippi River, prepared to fight to the death, but at the last minute, their seconds interrupted and stopped the duel.

That was the most lurid personal incident in Lincoln's life. It taught him an invaluable lesson in the art of dealing with people. Never again did he write an insulting letter. Never again did he ridicule anyone. And from that time on, he almost never criticized anybody for anything.

Time after time, during the Civil War, Lincoln put a new general at the head of the Army of the Potomac, and each one in turn—McClellan, Pope, Burnside, Hooker, Meade—blundered tragically and drove Lincoln to pacing the floor in despair. Half the nation savagely condemned these incompetent generals, but Lincoln, "with malice toward none, with charity for all," held his peace. One of his favorite quotations was "Judge not, that ye be not judged."

And when Mrs. Lincoln and others spoke harshly of the southern people, Lincoln replied: "Don't criticize them; they are just what we would be under similar circumstances."

Yet if any man ever had occasion to criticize, surely it was Lincoln.

Theodore Roosevelt said that when he, as president, was confronted with a perplexing problem, he used to lean back and look up at a large painting of Lincoln that hung above his desk in the White House and ask himself, "What would Lincoln do if he were in my shoes? How would he solve this problem?"

The next time we are tempted to admonish somebody, let's pull a five-dollar bill out of our pocket, look at Lincoln's picture on the bill, and ask, "How would Lincoln handle this problem if he had it?"

Mark Twain lost his temper occasionally and wrote letters that turned the paper brown. For example, he once wrote to a man who had aroused his ire: "The thing for you is a burial permit. You have only to speak and I will see that you get it." On another occasion he wrote to an editor about a proofreader's attempts to "improve my spelling and punctuation." He ordered: "Set the matter according to my copy hereafter and see that the proofreader retains his suggestions in the mush of his decayed brain."

The writing of these stinging letters made Mark Twain feel better. They allowed him to blow off steam, and the letters didn't do any real harm, because Mark's wife secretly lifted them out of the mail. They were never sent.

Do you know someone you would like to change and regulate and improve? Good! This is fine. I am all in favor of it. But why not begin on yourself? From a purely selfish standpoint, that is a lot more profitable than trying to improve others—yes, and a lot less dangerous. "Don't complain about the snow on your neighbor's roof," said Confucius, "when your own doorstep is unclean."

When I was still young and trying hard to impress people, I wrote a foolish letter to Richard Harding Davis, an author who once loomed large on the literary horizon of America. I was preparing a magazine article about authors, and I asked Davis to tell me about his method of work. A few weeks earlier, I had received a letter from someone with this notation at the bottom: "Dictated but not read." I was quite impressed. I felt that the writer must be very big and busy and important. I wasn't the slightest bit busy, but I was eager to make an impression on Richard Harding Davis, so I ended my short note with the words: "Dictated but not read."

He never troubled to answer the letter. He simply returned it to me with this scribbled across the bottom: "Your bad manners are exceeded only by your bad manners." True, I had blundered, and perhaps I deserved this rebuke. But, being human, I resented it. I resented it so sharply that when I read of the death of Richard Harding Davis ten years later, the one thought that still persisted in my mind—I am ashamed to admit—was the hurt he had given me.

If you and I want to stir up a resentment tomorrow that may rankle across the decades and endure until death, just let us indulge in a little stinging criticism.

When dealing with people, let us remember we are not dealing with creatures of logic. We are dealing with creatures of emotion, creatures bristling with prejudices and motivated by pride and vanity.

Bitter criticism caused the sensitive Thomas Hardy, one of the finest novelists ever to enrich English literature, to give up forever the writing of fiction. Criticism drove Thomas Chatterton, the English poet, to suicide.

Benjamin Franklin, tactless in his youth, became so diplomatic, so adroit at handling people, that he was made American ambassador to France. The secret of his success? "I will speak ill of no man," he said, "...and speak all the good I know of everybody."

Any fool can criticize, condemn, and complain—and most fools do.

But it takes character and self-control to be understanding and forgiving.

POINTS TO REMEMBER

1. The futility of criticism (if not done ethically).
2. Harsh criticism is the primary reason for unenthusiastic and unproductive employees.
3. If you ridicule someone, be ready to be ridiculed.

11

HOW TO INTEREST YOUR AUDIENCE

If you were invited to dine at the home of a rich man in certain sections of China, it would be proper to toss chicken bones and olive seeds over your shoulder on to the floor. You pay your host a compliment when you do that. You show that you realize that he is wealthy, that he has plenty of servants to tidy up after the meal. And he likes it.

You can be reckless with the remains of your sumptuous meal in a rich man's home, but in some parts of China the poorer people must save even the water they bathe in. To heat water costs so much that they must buy it at a hot-water shop. After they have bathed in it, they can take it back and sell it secondhand to the shopkeeper from whom they purchased it. When the second customer has soiled it, the water still retains a market value, although the price has softened a bit.

Have you found these facts about Chinese life interesting? If so, do you know why? Because those are very unusual aspects of very usual things. They are strange truths about such commonplace events as dining out and bathing.

That is what interests us—something new about the old.

Let us take another illustration. This page you are reading now, this sheet of paper you are looking at—it is very ordinary, isn't it? You have seen countless thousands of such pages. It seems dull and insipid now; but if I tell you a strange fact about it, you are almost sure to be interested. Let us see! This page seems like solid matter as you look at it now. But, in reality, it is more like a cobweb than solid matter. The physicist knows it is composed of atoms. And how small is an atom? There are as many atoms in one drop of water as there are drops of water in the Mediterranean Sea, that there are as many atoms in one drop of water as there are blades of grass in all the world. And the atoms that make this paper are composed of what? Still smaller things called electrons and protons. These electrons are all rotating around the central proton of the atom, as far from it, relatively speaking, as the moon is from the earth. And they are swinging through their orbits, these electrons of this tiny universe, at the inconceivable speed of approximately ten thousand miles a second. So the electrons that compose this sheet of paper you are holding have moved since you began reading this very sentence, a distance equal to that which stretches between New York and Tokyo....

And only two minutes ago you may have thought this piece of paper was still and dull and dead; but, in reality, it is one of God's mysteries. It is a veritable cyclone of energy.

If you are interested in it now, it is because you have learned a new and strange fact about it. There lies one of the secrets of interesting people. That is a significant truth, one that we ought to profit by in our every day intercourse. The entirely new is not interesting; the entirely old has no attractiveness for us. We want to be told something new about the old. You cannot, for example, interest a farmer with a description of the Cathedral at Bourges, or the Mona Lisa. They are too new to him. There is no tie-up to his old interests. But you can interest him by relating the fact that farmers in Holland till land below the level of the sea and dig ditches to act as fences and build bridges to serve as gates. Your farmer will listen open-mouthed while you tell him that Dutch farmers keep the cows, during the winter, under the same roof that houses the family, and sometimes the cows look out through lace curtains at driving snows. He knows about cows and fences—new slants, you see, on old things. "Lace curtains! For a cow!" he'll exclaim. "I'll be jiggered!" And he will retail that story to his friends.

Here is a talk delivered by a student of this course. As you read it, see if it interests you. If it does, do you know why?

HOW SULPHURIC ACID AFFECTS YOU

Most liquids are measured by the pint, quart, gallon or barrel. We ordinarily speak of quarts of wine, gallons of milk, and barrels of molasses. When a new oil gusher is discovered, we speak of its output as so many barrels per day. There is one liquid, however, that is manufactured and consumed in such large quantities that the unit of measurement employed is the ton. This liquid is sulphuric acid.

It touches you in your daily life in a score of ways. If it were not for sulphuric acid, your car would stop, and you would go back to "old Dobbin" and the buggy, for it is used extensively in the refining of parafine and petrol. The electric lights that illuminate your office, that shine upon your dinner table, that show you the way to bed at night, would not be possible without it.

When you get up in the morning and turn on the water for your bath, you use a nickel-plated tap, which requires sulphuric acid in its manufacture. It was required also in the finishing of your enamelled tub. The soap you use has possibly been made from greases or oils that have been treated with the acid... Your towel has made its acquaintance before you made the acquaintance of your towel. The bristles in your hairbrush have required it, and your celluloid comb could not have been produced without it. Your razor, no doubt, has been pickled in it after annealing.

You put on your underwear; you button up your outer garments. The bleacher, the manufacturer of dyes and the dyer himself used it. The button-maker possibly found the acid necessary to complete your buttons. The tanner used sulphuric acid in making the leather for your shoes, and it serves us again when we wish to polish them.

You come down to breakfast. The cup and saucer, if they be other than plain white, could not have come into being without it. It is used to produce the gilt and other ornamental colourings. Your spoon, knife and fork have seen a bath of sulphuric acid, if they be silver-plated.

The wheat of which your bread or rolls are made has possibly been grown by the use of a phosphate fertilizer, whose manufacture rests upon this acid.

And so on through the whole day, its work affects you at every turn. Go where you will, you cannot escape its influence. We can neither go to war without it nor live in peace without it. So it hardly seems possible that this acid, so essential to mankind, should be totally unfamiliar to the average man... But such is the case.

THE THREE MOST INTERESTING THINGS IN THE WORLD

What would you say they are—the three most interesting subjects in the world? Sex, property and religion. By the first we can create life, by the second we maintain it, by the third we hope to continue it in the world to come.

But it is *our* sex, *our* property, *our* religion that interests us. Our interests swarm about our own egos.

We are not interested in a talk on How to Make Wills in Peru; but we may be interested in a talk entitled "How to Make Our Wills". We are not interested—except, perhaps, out of curiosity—in the religion of the Hindoo; but we are vitally interested in a religion that insures *us* unending happiness in the world to come.

When the late Lord Northcliffe was asked what interests people, he answered with one word—and that word was "themselves". Northcliffe ought to have known for he was the wealthiest newspaper owner in Great Britain.

Do you want to know what kind of person you are? Ah, now we are on an interesting topic. We are talking about *you.* Here is a way for *you* to hold the mirror up to your real self, and see *you* as *you* really are. Watch your reveries. What do we mean by reveries? Let Professor James Harvey Robinson answer. We are quoting from *The Mind in the Making:*

> We all appear to ourselves to be thinking all the time during our waking hours, and most of us are aware that we go on thinking while we are asleep, even more foolishly than when awake. When uninterrupted by some practical issue we are engaged in what is known as a *reverie.* This is our spontaneous and favourite kind of thinking. We allow our ideas to take their own course and this course is determined by our hopes and fears, our spontaneous desires, their fulfilment or frustration, by our likes and dislikes, our loves and hates and resentments. *There is nothing else anything like so interesting to ourselves as*

> *ourselves.* All thought that is not more or less laboriously controlled and directed will inevitably circle about the beloved ego. It is amusing and pathetic to observe this tendency in ourselves and in others. We learn politely and generously to overlook this truth, but if we dare to think of it, it blazes forth like the noontide sun.
>
> Our reveries form the chief index of our fundamental character. They are a reflection of our nature as modified by often hidden and forgotten experiences...The reverie doubtless influences all our speculations in its persistent tendency to self-magnification and self-justification, which are its chief preoccupations.

So remember that the people you are to talk to spend most of their time when they are not concerned with the problems of business, in thinking about and justifying and glorifying themselves. Remember that the average man will be more concerned about the cook leaving than about Italy paying her debts. He will be more wrought up over a dull razor blade than over a revolution in South America. His own toothache will distress him more than an earthquake in Asia destroying half a million lives. He would rather listen to you say some nice thing about him than hear you discuss the ten greatest men in history.

HOW TO BE A GOOD CONVERSATIONALIST

The reason so many people are poor conversationalists is because they talk about only the things that interest them. That may be deadly boring to others. Reverse the process. Lead the other person into talking about *his* interests, *his* business, *his* golf score, *his* success—or, if it is a mother, *her* children. Do that and listen intently and you will give pleasure; consequently you will be considered a good conversationalist—even though you have done very little of the talking.

Mr. Harold Dwight recently made an extraordinarily successful speech at a banquet which marked the final session of a public speaking course. He talked about each man in turn around the entire table, told how he had talked when the course started, how he had improved; recalled the talks various members had made, the subjects they had discussed; he mimicked some of them, exaggerated their peculiarities, had everyone laughing, had everyone pleased. With such material, he could not possibly have failed. It was absolutely ideal. No other topic under the blue dome of Heaven would have so interested that group. Mr. Dwight knew how to handle human nature.

AN IDEA THAT WON TWO MILLION READERS

A few years ago, the *American Magazine* enjoyed an amazing growth. Its sudden leap in circulation became one of the sensations of the publishing world. The secret? The secret was the late John M. Siddall and his ideas. When I first met Siddall he had charge of the Interesting People Department of that periodical. I had written a few articles for him; and one day he sat down and talked to me for a long time.

"People are selfish," he said. "They are interested chiefly in themselves. They are not very much concerned about whether the government should own the railroads; but they do want to know how to get ahead, how to draw more salary, how to keep healthy. If I were editor of this magazine," he went on,

> I would tell them how to take care of their teeth, how to take baths, how to keep cool in summer, how to get a position, how to handle employees, how to buy homes,

> how to remember, how to avoid grammatical errors, and so on. People are always interested in human stories, so I would have some rich man tell how he made a million. I would get prominent bankers and presidents of various corporations to tell the stories of how they battled their ways up from the ranks to power and wealth.

Shortly after that, Siddall was made editor. The magazine then had a small circulation, and was comparatively a failure. Siddall did just what he said he would do. The response? It was overwhelming. The circulation figures climbed up to two hundred thousand, three, four, half a million.... Here was something the public wanted. Soon a million people a month were buying it, then a million and a half, finally two millions. It did not stop there, but continued to grow for many years. Siddall appealed to the selfish interests of his readers.

HOW DR. CONWELL INTERESTED MILLIONS OF HEARERS

What was the secret of the world's most popular lecture, "Acres of Diamonds"? Just the thing we have been talking about. John M. Siddall discussed this lecture in the conversation I have just referred to, and I think its enormous success had something to do with determining the policy of his magazine.

It tells people how they can get ahead, how they can make more out of themselves in their present environment.

It was never a static lecture. Dr. Conwell made it personal to each town where he spoke. That was of immense importance. The local references made it appear fresh and new. They made that town, that audience, seem important. Here is his own story of how he did it:

I visit a town or city, and try to arrive there early enough to see the postmaster, the barber, the keeper of the hotel, the principal of the schools, and the ministers of some of the churches, and then go into some of the factories and stores, and talk with the people, and get into sympathy with the local conditions of that town or city and see what has been their history, what opportunities they had, and what they had failed to do—and every town fails to do something—and then go to the lecture and talk to those people about the subjects which apply to their locality. Acres of Diamonds—the idea—has continuously been precisely the same. The idea is that in this country, every man has the opportunity to make more of himself than he does in his own environment, with his own skill, with his own energy, and with his own friends.

THE KIND OF SPEECH MATERIAL THAT ALWAYS HOLDS ATTENTION

You may possibly bore people if you talk about things and ideas, but you can hardly fail to hold their attention when you talk about people. Tomorrow there will be millions of conversations floating over fences in the backyards, over tea tables and dinner tables—and what will be the predominating note in most of them? Personalities. He said this. Mrs. So-and-so did that. I saw her doing this, that and the other. He is making a fortune, and so on.

I have addressed many gatherings of schoolchildren, and I soon learned by experience that in order to keep them interested I had to tell them stories about people. As soon as I became general and dealt with abstract ideas, Johnny became restless and wriggled in his seat, Tommy made a face at someone, Billy threw something across the aisle.

True, these were audiences of children; but the intelligence tests used in the army during the last war revealed the startling fact that 49 per cent of the people in the United States have a mental age of about thirteen. So one can hardly go wrong in making a generous use of human interest stories. Our magazines that are read by millions are filled with them.

I once asked a group of businessmen in Paris to talk on *How to Succeed.* Most of them praised the homely virtues, preached at, lectured to, and bored their hearers. (Incidentally, I recently heard one of the most prominent businessmen make this identical mistake in a radio talk on this identical topic.)

So I halted this class, and said something like this:

> We don't want to be lectured to. No one enjoys that. Remember you must be entertaining or we will pay no attention whatever to what you are saying. Also remember that one of the most interesting things in the world is sublimated, glorified gossip. So tell us the stories of two men you have known. Tell why one succeeded and why the other failed. We will gladly listen to that, remember it and possibly profit by it. It will also, by the way, be far easier for you to deliver than are these wordy, abstract preachments.

There was a certain member of that course who invariably found it difficult to interest either himself or his audience. This night, however, he seized the human story suggestion, and told us of two of his classmates in college. One of them had been so conservative that he had bought shirts at the different stores in town, and made charts showing which ones laundered best, wore longest and gave the most service for the money invested. His mind was always on pennies; yet, when he graduated—from an engineering college—he had such a high opinion of his own importance that he was not willing to begin at the bottom and work his way up, as the other graduates were doing. Even when the third annual reunion of the class came, he was still making laundry charts of his shirts, while waiting for some extraordinarily good thing to come his way. It never came. A quarter of a century has passed since then, and this man, dissatisfied and soured, still holds a minor position.

The speaker then contrasted with this failure the story of one of his classmates who had surpassed all expectations. This particular chap was a good mixer. Everyone liked him. Although he was ambitious to do big things later, he started as a draughtsman. But he was always on the lookout for opportunity. Plans were then being made for an exposition. He knew engineering talent would be needed there, so he resigned from his position and moved to the town of the exhibition. Through his agreeable personality, he soon won the friendship of a man with considerable influence. The two formed a partnership, and engaged immediately in the contracting business. They did considerable work for the telephone company, and this man was finally taken over by that concern at a large salary. Today he is a multimillionaire, one of the principal owners of Western Union.

We have recorded here only the bare outline of what the speaker told. He made his talk interesting and illuminating with a score of amusing and human details... He talked on and on—this man who could not ordinarily find material for a three minute speech—and he was surprised beyond words to learn when he stopped that he had held the floor on this occasion for half an hour. The speech had been so interesting that it seemed short to everyone. It was this student's first real triumph.

Almost every student can profit by this incident. The average speech would be far more appealing if it were rich and replete with human interest stories. The speaker ought to attempt to make only a few points and to illustrate them with concrete cases. Such a method of speech building can hardly fail to get and hold attention.

If possible, these stories ought to tell of struggles, of things fought for and victories won. All of us are tremendously interested in fights and combats. There is an old saying that all the world loves a lover. It doesn't. What all the world loves is a scrap. It wants to see two lovers struggling for the hand of one woman. As an illustration of this fact, read almost any novel, magazine story, or go to see almost any film drama. When all the obstacles are removed and the reputed hero takes the so-called heroine in his arms, the audience begins reaching for their hats and coats. Five minutes later the sweeping women are gossiping over their broom handles.

Almost all magazine fiction is based on this formula. Make the reader like the hero or heroine. Make him or her long for something intensely. Make that something seem impossible to get. Show how the hero or heroine fights and gets it.

The story of how a man battled in business or profession against discouraging odds and won is always inspiring, always interesting. A magazine editor once told me that the real, inside story of any person's life is entertaining. If one has struggled and fought—and who hasn't—his story, if correctly told, will appeal. There can be no doubt of that.

BE CONCRETE

The writer once had in the same course in public speaking, a Doctor of Philosophy and a rough-and-ready fellow who had spent his youth thirty years ago in the British Navy. The polished scholar was a university professor; his classmate from the seven seas was the proprietor of a small side street moving-van establishment. Strange to say, the moving-van man's talks during the course would have held a popular audience far better than the talks of the college professor. Why? The college man spoke in beautiful English, with a demeanour of culture and refinement, and with logic and clearness; but his talks lacked one essential, *concreteness.* They were too vague, too general. On the other hand, the van owner possessed hardly enough power of cerebration to generalize. When he talked he got right down to business immediately. He was definite; he was concrete. That quality, coupled with his virility and his fresh phraseology, made his talks very entertaining.

I have cited this instance, not because it is typical either of college men or moving-van proprietors, but because it illustrates the interest-getting power that accrues to the man—regardless of education—who has the happy habit of being concrete and definite in his speaking.

This principle is so important that we are going to use several illustrations to try to lodge it firmly in your mind. We hope you will never forget it, never neglect it.

Is it, for example, more interesting to state that Martin Luther, as a boy, was "stubborn and intractable", or is it better to say that he confessed that his teachers had flogged him as often as "fifteen times in a forenoon"?

Words like "stubborn and intractable" have very little attention value. But isn't it easy to listen to the flogging count?

The old method of writing a biography was to deal in a lot of generalities which Aristotle called, and rightly called, "The refuge of weak minds." The new method is to deal with concrete facts that speak for themselves. The old-fashioned biographer said that John Doe was born of "poor but honest parents". The new method would say that John Doe's father couldn't afford a pair of overshoes, so when the snow came, he had to tie gunny sacking around his shoes to keep his feet dry and warm; but, in spite of his poverty, he never watered the milk and he never traded a horse with the heaves as a sound animal. That shows that his parents were "poor but honest", doesn't it? And doesn't it do it in a way that is far more interesting than the "poor but honest" method?

If this method works for modern biographers it will work also for modern speakers.

Let us take one more illustration. Suppose you wished to state that the potential horse power wasted at Niagara every day was appalling. Suppose you said just that, and then added, that if it were utilized and the resulting profits turned to purchasing the necessities of life, crowds could be clothed and fed. Would that be the way to make it interesting and entertaining? No—No. Isn't this far better? We are quoting from Edwin E. Slosson in the *Daily Science News Bulletin:*

> We are told that there are some millions of people in poverty and poorly nourished in this country, yet here at Niagara is wasted the equivalent of 250,000 loaves of bread an hour. We may see with our mind's eye 600,000 nice fresh eggs dropping over the precipice every hour and making a gigantic omelette in the whirlpool. If calico were continuously pouring from the looms in a stream 4,000 feet wide like Niagara River, it would represent the same destruction of property. If a Carnegie Library were held under the spout it would be filled with good books in an hour or two. Or we can imagine a big department store floating down from Lake Erie every day and smashing its

varied contents on the rocks 160 feet below. That would be an exceedingly interesting and diverting spectacle, quite as attractive to the crowd as the present, and no more expensive to maintain. Yet some people might object to that on the ground of extravagance who now object to the utilization of the power of the falling water.

PICTURE-BUILDING WORDS

In this process of interest-getting, there is one aid, one technique, that is of the highest importance; yet it is all but ignored. The average speaker does not seem to be aware of its existence. He has probably never consciously thought about it at all. I refer to the process of using words that create pictures. The speaker who is easy to listen to is the one who sets images floating before your eyes. The one who employs foggy, commonplace, colorless symbols sets the audience to nodding.

Pictures. Pictures. Pictures. They are as free as the air you breathe. Sprinkle them through your talks, your conversation, and you will be more entertaining, more influential.

To illustrate, let us take the excerpt just quoted from the *Daily Science News Bulletin* regarding Niagara. Look at the picture words. They leap up and go scampering away in every sentence, as thick as rabbits in Australia: "250,000 loaves of bread, 600,000 eggs dropping over the precipice, gigantic omelette in the whirlpool, calico pouring from the looms in a stream 4,000 feet wide, Carnegie library held under the spout, books, a big department store floating, smashing, rocks below, falling water."

It would be almost as difficult to ignore such a talk or article as it would be to pay not the slightest attention to the scenes from a film unwinding on the silver screen of the motion picture theatre.

Picture-building phrases swarm through the pages of the Bible and through Shakespeare like bees around a cider mill. For example, a commonplace writer would have said that a certain thing would be superfluous, like trying to improve the perfect. How did Shakespeare express the same thought? With a picture phrase that is immortal: "To gild refined gold, to paint the lily, to throw perfume on the violet."

Did you ever pause to observe that the proverbs that are passed on from generation to generation are almost all visual sayings? "A bird in the hand is worth two in the bush." "It never rains but it pours." "You can lead a horse to water but you can't make him drink." And you will find the same picture element in almost all the similes that have lived for centuries and grown hoary with too much use: "Sly as a fox." "Dead as a door nail." "Flat as a pancake." "Hard as a rock."

Lincoln continually talked in visual terminology. When he became annoyed with the long, complicated, red-tape reports that came to his desk in the White House, he objected to them, not with a colorless phraseology, but with a picture phrase that it is almost impossible to forget. "When I send a man to buy a horse," said he, "I don't want to be told how many hairs the horse has in his tail. I wish only to know his points."

THE INTEREST-GETTING VALUE OF CONTRASTS

Listen to the following condemnation of Charles I by Macaulay.

Note that Macaulay not only uses pictures, but he also employs balanced sentences. Violent contrasts almost always hold our interests; violent contrasts are the very brick and mortar of this paragraph:

> We charge him with having broken his coronation oath; and we are told that he kept his marriage vow! We accuse him of having given up his people to the merciless inflictions of the most hot-headed of prelates; and the defence is that he took his little son on his knee and kissed him! We censure him for having violated the articles of the Petition of Right, after having, for good and valuable consideration, promised to observe them; and we are informed that he was accustomed to hear prayers at six o'clock in the morning! It is to such considerations as these, together with his Vandyke dress, his handsome face and his peaked beard, that he owes, we verily believe, most of his popularity with the present generation.

INTEREST IS CONTAGIOUS

We have been discussing so far the kind of material that interests an audience. However, one might mechanically follow all the suggestions made here and speak according to Cocker, and yet be vapid and dull. Catching and holding the interest of people is a delicate thing, a matter of feeling and spirit. It is not like operating a steam engine. No book of precise rules can be given for it.

Interest, be it remembered, is contagious. Your hearers are almost sure to catch it if you have a bad case of it yourself. A short time ago, a gentleman rose during a session of this course and warned his audience that if the present methods of catching rock fish were continued, the species would become extinct. And in a very few years! He felt his subject. It was important. He was in real earnest about it. Everything about his matter and manner showed that. When he arose to speak, I did not know that there was such an animal as a rock fish. I imagine that most of the audience shared my lack of knowledge and lack of interest. But before the speaker finished, all of us had caught something of his concern. All of us would probably have been willing to have signed a petition to the legislature to protect the rock fish by law.

I once asked Richard Washburn Child, then American Ambassador to Italy, the secret of his success as an interesting writer. He replied: "I am so excited about life that I cannot keep still. I just have to tell people about it." One cannot keep from being enthralled with a speaker or writer like that.

I recently went to hear a speaker in London: after he was through, one of our party, the late E.F. Benson, a well-known English novelist, remarked that he enjoyed the last part of the talk far more than the first. When I asked him why, he replied: "The speaker himself seemed more interested in the last part, and I always rely on the speaker to supply the enthusiasm and interest."

POINTS TO REMEMBER

1. There is nothing else as interesting to us as ourselves.
2. The secret of a good conversationalist is that he shows interest in others.
3. A "rags to riches" story will always engage the audience.

12

SEEING THINGS FROM THE OTHER PERSON'S POINT OF VIEW

Long before ad man Burt Manning ever set foot on Madison Avenue, he wanted to be a writer. Not a copywriter, an author. So young Manning slaved over a typewriter every day, producing short stories and novels and what he was sure were gut-wrenching plays. But like most young writers, Manning couldn't come close to supporting himself with his words. He needed a job to pay the bills.

Door-to-door selling was the best idea he could find.

He sold *Encyclopaedia Britannicas*. He sold high-end kitchenware. He even went door-to-door in the old working-class neighborhoods of his native Chicago, selling cemetery property.

That last product turned out to be the most profitable of all—but not at first. It wasn't for lack of trying. Every evening after a full day at the typewriter, Manning put on a suit and tie. He packed his salesman's case. And he pressed his most enthusiastic cemetery pitch on the people who answered his knocks: how cemetery property offered strong investment advantages, how Chicago's rapid population growth would surely produce a scarcity of cemetery property, how his company's five-year buy-back guarantee made this a no-risk deal.

"It was actually a very good, low-cost investment, and I believed in it. But I couldn't sell a thing. I wasn't coming at it from their point of view. Instead of focusing on their most important concerns, I kept focusing on the financial aspects. But with the product I was selling, there was something much more relevant that I hadn't thought about."

Manning had failed to ask himself the most basic questions. "I had to say, 'What's really of concern to these folks? What separates them in their views from other people I might know? What do I have to offer that will make them feel good about themselves and feel good about what they are doing for their families?'"

Once asked, these questions were easy enough to answer.

"This was Back of the Yards, a very close-knit ethnic neighborhood," Manning recalls. "Family unit was extremely important. People were close to their families—cousins, grandparents, uncles, aunts. People stayed close. They did not want to leave the neighborhood."

Even after death, Manning guessed. So instead of talking investment and finance, Manning figured he should be talking family and neighborhood and staying close to home. That cemetery property, he says looking back, "really did provide them with an opportunity, if they wanted it, to have the whole family unit be close in a burial place that they could visit easily, instead of having to go two hundred miles out of town to visit the grandfather or great-grandfather's plot. Those were very important issues to these folks.

"I didn't really understand that at first," Manning says. "All I knew was that I was offering a very good investment at a reasonable cost, but they weren't interested. They wouldn't buy that kind of product for that reason.

"Once I understood what they really cared about, what they wanted, and showed them how easily they could have it," Manning recalls, "I did quite well."

Manning, who went on to a hugely successful career as head of the J. Walter Thompson advertising agency, was lucky to learn that lesson so early in life: *Look at things from the other person's point of view.* It's the single most important key to getting along in the world.

For Manning, the other person was that Chicago housewife and her husband. But the other person could just as easily be the boss, the coworker, the employee, the customer, the spouse, the friend, or the child. It could be anyone, really. The basic principle—always try to look at things from the other person's perspective—applies just as well.

"There's going to be much more demand on leaders of the future," predicts Bill Makahilahila, Director of Human Resources at SGS-Thomson, a worldwide semiconductor producer. "I don't care whether you're a janitor or a receptionist. You've got to learn how to get along with people. If you think having position gives you the authority to ride over people, it's not true anymore. You're going to have to start thinking in terms of the interests of others."

Once that process gets going inside a company, Makahilahila has observed, a whole new kind of communication results. "If you learn to think in terms of the interests of your boss, now you're starting on the same basis. You begin to have an open dialogue. Don't think only of yourself. Don't think only of your own needs. Think about George's needs here. Or Sandy's needs there. And think about what kinds of questions you would ask to draw them out, to understand their needs."

The results can be remarkable in your personal relationships as well. "Recently my four-year-old grandson, Jordan, spent the night with Maxine and me," says Vern L. Laun, a prominent Phoenix businessman. "When Jordan woke up on Friday morning, I had the news on the TV, and I was reading the newspaper. Jordan saw I wasn't really listening to the news, and he wanted to watch cartoons.

"Jordan said to me, 'Gwampa,'—he can't say Grandpa—'would you like me to shut off the TV so you can enjoy the newspaper?' I sensed that he wanted to watch cartoons. So I said, 'Go ahead and shut it off. Or watch something else if you would like.'

"In a matter of seconds, he had the remote control. He was on the floor and changing to a channel with cartoons. At age four, he first thought, 'What does Gwampa want, so I can get what I want?'"

Barbara Hayes, the vice president of marketing for Lerner New York, a division of The Limited, Inc., is almost obsessive when it comes to this approach. In her case—as with many retail-business people—the other person is the customer.

The process, as far as Hayes is concerned, begins before a potential customer even steps inside a Lerner store. "In some malls we have seventy-foot lease fronts," she said. "The customer, within eight-point-five seconds, is going to decide whether to walk into that store or just go past it." That instant decision, multiplied millions of times, will determine in large measure whether Lerner is a success. Or as Hayes looks at it, "I've got eight-point-five seconds."

THE CUSTOMER GETS THE LAST WORD

The highly competitive retailing industry has really been the leader in seeing the world from the customer's point of view.

We've all been inside a poorly run store. All the clerks

are huddled together, talking to each other. An approaching customer feels like an intruder in some private club. Service? You want service? The sales clerks are far too bored, far too annoyed, or far too busy to be interrupted for something like that.

The era of apathetic customer service has finally begun to pass. Customers said enough. Stores that don't adapt to the new customer-is-everything ethic tend now to go out of business fast, taking their aloof employees with them.

The late Sam Walton hired full-time "greeters" for his Wal-Mart discount stores, people whose sole job was to stand near the front door, say hello to customers, and point them in the right direction. Why? It wasn't just Walton's Arkansas hospitality. He had enough sense to see his own business as the customers do. Here they are, stepping into this huge, brightly lit store, with aisle after aisle of merchandise and no idea which way to go. People need guidance. They appreciate the store that provides it. And if they can locate the merchandise that they're looking for, they are more likely to buy it. That'll delight the customers, which will be good for the store. A delighted customer is good for any store.

"Exceed your customers' expectations." That was always one of Sam Walton's rules. "If you do, they'll come back over and over. Give them what they want and a little more."

At retailing's upper end, the Nordstrom chain managed to sail through the recession of the late 1980s and the early 1990s. The department store's number-one priority: see things the customer's way.

"Nordstrom is the most feared retailer in the world," says business consultant Denis E. Waitley. "My wife, Susan, has discovered them as her greatest ally. She bought two pairs of Nordstrom shoes and took them back after she wore them for two weeks. One of the pair hurt, and they took them both back. No problem. Can do. The customer is always king and queen. Customers are royalty, treated the way we want to be treated. That's the way it works."

Even so, Waitley wasn't prepared for the early evening phone call he got at home one night.

A friendly-sounding woman was on the line.

She: "Hello, may I speak to Susan Waitley, please? This is Martha, your Nordstrom customer-service representative."

He: "Martha, you're a commissioned sales rep trying to make extra points. What do you want? I'm getting ready to eat, and I don't allow interruptions during dinner. What is it you want Susan for?"

She: "The shoes came in at the store in Susan's size and color, and I'm delivering them after work."

He: "As I remember, you live in South County. We're in North County, which is out of your way. I'll be eating in five minutes, which won't allow you enough time to come by. But thank you for trying."

She: "I'm calling from my cellular phone in your driveway."

He: "Oh, come on in."

So Nordstrom made a sale, and even Waitley had to admit he was impressed. The store was looking at things in terms of the customer's interests.

It isn't How can we do business in a manner most convenient to us, it is How can we do business in the way most convenient to you. Delighting the customer—that's what it's all about. And there's no way to make all those judgments without looking through the potential customer's eyes.

For every product it sells, Dun & Bradstreet Software Services, Inc., creates a "customer council."

"We do not build a product until the customer council has

instructed us that this is their priority," explains John Imlay, the company's chairman. "They come with a priority list. We come with one, the features and functions. We want to be competitive and they want to satisfy their needs. They give us input and we take pride in solving their problems and satisfying their needs."

This is not considered a luxury at Dun & Bradstreet. It's a basic part of doing business. "We could not develop a product without customer input," Imlay declares. "There would be an ivory tower, and then we'd be no good."

This outward-looking perspective shouldn't be reserved only for customers. It applies as well to employees, to suppliers, to anyone else you come into contact with every day.

David Holman runs the export division of John Holman & Co. Pty. Ltd., an Australian produce vendor. One day Holman had the unhappy task of calling up one of his biggest growers with a piece of terrible news: the new export price for the man's vegetables was going to be half what was originally expected.

This generated the predictable reaction on the phone. The man sounded aghast. The situation seemed serious enough that Holman decided to drive the two hours to the man's farm and finish the discussion in person.

When he got to the farm, the fields were wet and muddy, and the grower was out with the crop. So Holman borrowed a spare pair of the grower's rubber boots and marched out to meet him in the field.

"How are you doing?" Holman asked the grower in a concerned tone of voice.

Then he listened with true empathy about all the hard work the grower had put in, about the time that had gone into this year's crop, about the economic hardship of being on the land in the 1990s, about his disappointment over the current price.

Holman had no trouble understanding the grower's point

of view. The grower clearly had major problems on his hands. Holman just expressed a warm personal concern. That was enough. Much to Holman's surprise, without his even mentioning the price he had offered or talking about the purchase of the crop, the grower said, "I can see you are being genuine with me, and you understand my position. I will accept your offer in the hope that things will improve soon for us both."

So get into the other person's boots. There's no better way to ease a difficult situation.

"We have a little carpet venture in China," says Adriana Bitter, president of Scalamandré Silks. "On the day of the Tiananmen Square massacre, when nothing was operating for big business, our little mill was. That day we sent off a telegram, saying we were terribly sorry they were suffering. We never mentioned the giant order that had to be delivered to England the following week. We thought, 'No way. Nothing's getting out.' But we received an answer, 'Thank you for your telegram. Your order was shipped this morning.' I don't know how they got it out of China, but they did. We have a good rapport with this little mill out in the mountains."

By seeing things from the mill workers' point of view, Bitter made sure the impossible order arrived.

This obsessive attention to customer service is a life-or-death issue in every business. At Harrison Conference Services, Inc., if it means making the facilities more comfortable for women or serving a more healthful menu, no problem. Can do.

And it's not enough just to wait around for the suggestion box to fill up or the complaint letters to arrive in the mail. It's vital to stay one step ahead of the customers. Smart business leaders are always thinking about what the customer will want next—a few days, a few weeks, a few months from now. This is all part of thinking in terms of the other person's interests, a reversal of What's in it for me?

There's certainly no shortage of business publications being sold today—magazines, books, newsletters, on-line data services, fax reports—but the vast majority of these publications, Martin Edelston believed, were not delivering the practical information that many business people craved. "They're devoted to business news, more or less. But they don't tell you, in practical terms, how to deal with your employees, how to cut health costs. They'll talk about the healthcare problem, but they won't tell you how to dig into it." So Edelston started a company, *Boardroom Reports*, to fill that void.

Does it take a genius to dream up this stuff? Hardly. It takes leaders who are asking themselves day in and day out, "How does the customer rate our business? What will the customer want next?"

Just about every business can benefit from looking at the world this way.

"Last year," says SAS Airlines president Jan Carlzon, "each of our ten million customers came in contact with approximately five SAS employees. This contact lasted an average of fifteen seconds. These fifty million moments of truth are moments that ultimately determine whether SAS will succeed."

Looking at things from the other person's perspective doesn't happen on its own. The questions aren't complicated, but they have to be asked. Ask them at work, at home, in the social scene. You'll soon be seeing things as others do.

What life experiences does the other person bring to this interaction? What is the other person trying to achieve here? What is the other person trying to avoid? What other constituencies does the other person have to serve? What will it take for the other person to consider this encounter a success?

The answers to these various questions will be different at

different companies, although some themes will no doubt recur. But whatever the precise answers, the point here isn't simply to go along with everything the other person wants. It is to make a genuine, sincere effort to figure out what the other person is really looking for—and as much as is humanly possible, to deliver that. If you can help people solve their problems, the world is your oyster.

It took an angry complaint letter to remind Corning's David Luther that his idea of great isn't necessarily the customer's idea of great. Luther was working in Britain in those days. Corning had sent around a comprehensive customer survey, and this one respondent did not mince words. "Corning stinks," he wrote.

As any good executive would, Luther followed up on the complaint and invited the man in for a chat. "Well, why does Corning stink?" Luther asked the man, who worked in a warehouse that was stocked with Corning products.

"It's your labels," the man said.

"Ah, I got you," Luther said, brightening up. "You've got to be confusing us with somebody else. Our labels are printed by computer. They show the source of manufacturing, the country of origin, your code, our code, the date, everything you want to know."

The man shook his head slowly back and forth. "Son," he asked, "have you ever been in a warehouse?"

"Well, yeah," Luther answered. "I spent ten years in a warehouse, as a matter of fact."

"Have you ever been to my warehouse?" Luther admitted he hadn't. "Come with me," the man told him.

So the two of them marched directly to the warehouse. The tiers in this particular warehouse were higher than those Luther was used to back home. The upper tiers, in fact, were way up above Luther's head.

The warehouse man directed his attention to one of the top shelves. "We put Corning stuff up there," the man said. "But can you read the labels up there?"

"No," Luther had to admit. "I can't, as a matter of fact."

"That's the point," the warehouse man told him. "Can't see it." So that's what he meant by "Corning stinks."

Luther learned a valuable lesson that day. "You've got to get inside the customer's organization," he said. "Think about the person in the warehouse. He's got requirements. She's got requirements." And you won't find out about them unless you bother to ask.

If you want to have more successful relationships with your customers, your family, and your friends, look at things from the other person's perspective.

POINTS TO REMEMBER

1. Try to figure out your unique trait.
2. Start to see things from multiple perspectives.
3. Don't aspire to meet your audience's expectations. Exceed them.

13

HOW TO DEAL WITH PEOPLE

There is only one way under high heaven to get anybody to do anything. Did you ever stop to think of that? Yes, just one way. And that is by making the other person want to do it.

Remember, there is no other way.

Of course, you can make someone want to give you his watch by sticking a revolver in his ribs. You can make your employees give you cooperation—until your back is turned—by threatening to fire them. You can make a child do what you want it to do by a whip or a threat. But these crude methods have sharply undesirable repercussions.

The only way I can get you to do anything is by giving you what you want.

What do you want?

Sigmund Freud said that everything you and 1 do springs from two motives: the sex urge and the desire to be great.

John Dewey, one of America's most profound philosophers, phrased it a bit differently. Dr. Dewey said that the deepest urge in human nature is "the desire to be important." Remember that phrase: "the desire to be important." It is significant. You are going to hear a lot about it in this book.

What do you want? Not many things, but the few things that you do wish, you crave with an insistence that will not be denied. Some of the things most people want include:

1. Health and the preservation of life
2. Food
3. Sleep
4. Money and the things money will buy
5. Life in the hereafter
6. Sexual gratification
7. The well-being of our children
8. A feeling of importance

Almost all these wants are usually gratified—all except one. But there is one longing—almost as deep, almost as imperious, as the desire for food or sleep—that is seldom gratified. It is what Freud calls "the desire to be great." It is what Dewey calls "the desire to be important."

Lincoln once began a letter saying: "Everybody likes a compliment." William James said: "The deepest principle in human nature is the craving to be appreciated." He didn't speak, mind you, of the "wish" or the "desire" or the "longing" to be appreciated. He said the "craving" to be appreciated.

Here is a gnawing and unfaltering human hunger, and the rare individual who honestly satisfies this heart hunger will hold people in the palm of his or her hand and "even the undertaker will be sorry when he dies."

The desire for a feeling of importance is one of the chief distinguishing differences between mankind and the animals. To illustrate: When I was a farm boy out in Missouri, my father bred fine Duroc-Jersey hogs and pedigreed white-faced cattle. We used to exhibit our hogs and white-faced cattle at the country fairs and livestock shows throughout the Middle West. We won first prizes by the score. My father pinned his blue ribbons on a sheet of white muslin, and when friends or visitors came to the house, he would get out the long sheet of muslin. He would hold one end and I would hold the other while he exhibited the blue ribbons.

The hogs didn't care about the ribbons they had won. But Father did. These prizes gave him a feeling of importance.

If our ancestors hadn't had this flaming urge for a feeling of importance, civilization would have been impossible. Without it, we should have been just about like animals.

It was this desire for a feeling of importance that inspired Dickens to write his immortal novels. This desire inspired Sir Christopher Wren to design his symphonies in stone. This desire made Rockefeller amass millions that he never spent! And this same desire made the richest family in your town build a house far too large for its requirements.

This desire makes you want to wear the latest styles, drive the latest cars, and talk about your brilliant children.

History sparkles with amusing examples of famous people struggling for a feeling of importance. Even George Washington wanted to be called "His Mightiness, the President of the United States"; and Columbus pleaded for the title "Admiral of the Ocean and Viceroy of India." Catherine the Great refused to open letters that were not addressed to "Her Imperial Majesty"; and Mrs. Lincoln, in the White House, turned upon Mrs. Grant like a tigress and shouted, "How dare you be seated in my presence until I invite you!"

APPRECIATION AS A COPING MECHANISM

People sometimes become invalids in order to win sympathy and attention, and get a feeling of importance. For example, take Mrs. McKinley. She got a feeling of importance by forcing her husband, the president of the United States, to neglect important affairs of state while he reclined on the bed beside her for hours at a time, his arm about her, soothing her to sleep. She fed her gnawing desire for attention by insisting that he remain with her while she was having her teeth fixed, and once created a stormy scene when he had to leave her alone with the dentist while he kept an appointment with John Hay, his secretary of state.

The writer Mary Roberts Rinehart once told me of a bright, vigorous young woman who became an invalid in order to get a feeling of importance. "One day," said Mrs. Rinehart, "this woman had been obliged to face something, her age perhaps. The lonely years were stretching ahead and there was little left for her to anticipate.

"She took to her bed; and for ten years her old mother traveled to the third floor and back, carrying trays, nursing her. Then one day the old mother, weary with service, lay down and died. For some weeks, the invalid languished; then she got up, put on her clothing, and resumed living again."

Some authorities declare that people may actually go insane in order to find, in the dreamland of insanity, the feeling of importance that has been denied them in the harsh world of reality. There are more patients suffering from mental diseases in the United States than from all other diseases combined.

What is the cause of insanity?

Nobody can answer such a sweeping question, but we know that certain diseases, such as syphilis, break down and destroy the brain cells and result in insanity. In fact, about one-half of all mental diseases can be attributed to such physical causes as brain lesions, alcohol, toxins, and injuries. But the other half—and this is the appalling part of the story—the other half of the people who go insane apparently have nothing organically wrong with their brain cells. In post-mortem examinations, when their brain tissues are studied under the highest-powered microscopes, these tissues are found to be apparently just as healthy as yours and mine.

Why do these people go insane?

I put that question to the head physician of one of our most important psychiatric hospitals. This doctor, who has received the highest honors and the most coveted awards for his knowledge of this subject, told me frankly that he didn't know why people went insane. Nobody knows for sure. But he did say that many people who go insane find in insanity a feeling of importance that they were unable to achieve in the world of reality. Then he told me this story:

"I have a patient right now whose marriage proved to be a tragedy. She wanted love, sexual gratification, children, and social prestige, but life blasted all her hopes. Her husband didn't love her. He refused even to eat with her and forced her to serve his meals in his room upstairs. She had no children, no social standing. She went insane; and, in her imagination, she divorced her husband and resumed her maiden name. She now believes she has married into English aristocracy, and she insists on being called Lady Smith.

"And as for children, she imagines now that she has had a new child every night. Each time I call on her she says: 'Doctor, I had a baby last night.'"

Life once wrecked all her dream ships on the sharp rocks of reality; but in the sunny, fantasy isles of insanity, all her barkentines race into port with canvas billowing and winds singing through the sails.

Tragic? Oh, I don't know. Her physician said to me: "If I could stretch out my hand and restore her sanity, I wouldn't do it. She's much happier as she is."

If some people are so hungry for a feeling of importance

that they actually go insane to get it, imagine what miracle you and I can achieve by giving people honest appreciation this side of insanity.

We nourish the bodies of our children and friends and employees, but how often do we nourish their self-esteem? We provide them with roast beef and potatoes to build energy, but we neglect to give them kind words of appreciation that would sing in their memories for years like the music of the morning stars.

Flattery seldom works with discerning people. It is shallow, selfish, and insincere. It ought to fail and it usually does. True, some people are so hungry, so thirsty, for appreciation that they will swallow anything, just as a starving man will eat grass and fishworms.

Even Queen Victoria was susceptible to flattery. Prime Minister Benjamin Disraeli confessed that he laid it on thick in dealing with the queen. To use his exact words, he said he "spread it on with a trowel." But Disraeli was one of the most polished, deft, and adroit men who ever ruled the far-flung British Empire. He was a genius in his line. What would work for him wouldn't necessarily work for you and me. In the long run, flattery will do you more harm than good. Flattery is counterfeit, and like counterfeit money, it will eventually get you into trouble if you pass it to someone else.

The difference between appreciation and flattery? That is simple. One is sincere and the other insincere. One comes from the heart out; the other from the teeth out. One is unselfish; the other selfish. One is universally admired; the other universally condemned.

I recently saw a bust of the Mexican hero General Álvaro Obregón in the Chapultepec palace in Mexico City. Below the bust are carved these wise words from General Obregón's philosophy: "Don't be afraid of enemies who attack you. Be afraid of friends who flatter you."

No! No! No! I am not suggesting flattery? Far from it. I'm talking about a new way of life. Let me repeat. *I am talking about a new way of life.*

King George V had a set of six maxims displayed on the walls of his study at Buckingham Palace. One of these maxims said: "Teach me neither to proffer nor receive cheap praise." That's all flattery is—cheap praise. I once read a definition of flattery that may be worth repeating: "Flattery is telling the other person precisely what he thinks about himself."

"Use what language you will," said Ralph Waldo Emerson, "you can never say anything but what you are."

If all we had to do was flatter, everybody would catch on and we should all be experts in human relations.

When we are not engaged in thinking about some definite problem, we usually spend about ninety-five percent of our time thinking about ourselves. Now, if we stop thinking about ourselves for a while and begin to think of the other person's good points, we won't have to resort to flattery so cheap and false that it can be spotted almost before it is out of the mouth.

One of the most neglected virtues of our daily existence is appreciation. Somehow, we neglect to praise our son or daughter when he or she brings home a good report card, and we fail to encourage our children when they first succeed in baking a cake or building a birdhouse. Nothing pleases children more than this kind of parental interest and approval.

The next time you enjoy filet mignon at the club, send word to the chef that it was excellently prepared, and when a tired salesperson shows you unusual courtesy, please mention it.

Every minister, lecturer, and public speaker knows the discouragement of pouring himself or herself out to an audience and not receiving a single ripple of appreciative comment. What applies to professionals applies doubly to workers in offices, shops, and factories, and to our families and friends. In our interpersonal relations we should never forget that all our associates are human beings and hunger for appreciation. It is the legal tender that all souls enjoy.

Try leaving a friendly trail of little sparks of gratitude on your daily trips. You will be surprised how they will set small flames of friendship that will be rose beacons on your next visit.

Pamela Dunham of New Fairfield, Connecticut, had among her responsibilities on her job the supervision of a janitor who was doing a very poor job. The other employees would jeer at him and litter the hallways to show him what a bad job he was doing. It was so bad, productive time was being lost in the shop.

Without success, Pam tried various ways to motivate this person. She noticed that occasionally he did a particularly good piece of work. She made a point to praise him for it in front of the other people. Each day the job he did all around got better, and pretty soon he started doing all his work efficiently. Now he does an excellent job and other people give him appreciation and recognition. Honest appreciation got results where criticism and ridicule failed.

Hurting people not only does not change them, it is never called for. There is an old saying that I have cut out and pasted on my mirror, where I cannot help but see it every day:

> I shall pass this way but once; any good, therefore, that I can do or any kindness that I can show to any human being, let me do it now. Let me not defer nor neglect it, for I shall not pass this way again.

Emerson said: "Every man I meet is my superior in some way. In that, I learn of him."

If that was true of Emerson, isn't it likely to be a thousand times more true of you and me? Let's cease thinking of our accomplishments, our wants. Let's try to figure out the other person's good points. Then forget flattery. Give honest, sincere appreciation. Be "hearty in your approbation and lavish in your praise," and people will cherish your words and treasure them and repeat them over a lifetime—repeat them years after you have forgotten them.

POINTS TO REMEMBER

1. The desire for a feeling of importance is one of the chief distinguishing differences between mankind and animals.
2. Nourishing mental health is just as important as nourishing physical health.
3. Sincere appreciation is a powerful medicine.

14

AFTER-DINNER AND OTHER OCCASIONAL SPEAKING

Perhaps the most brilliant, and certainly the most entertaining, of all speeches are those delivered on after-dinner and other special occasions. The air of well-fed content in the former, and of expectancy well primed in the latter, furnishes an audience which, though not readily won, is prepared for the best, while the speaker himself is pretty sure to have been chosen for his gifts of oratory.

The first essential of good occasional speaking is to study the occasion. Precisely what is the object of the meeting? How important is the occasion to the audience? How large will the audience be? What sort of people are they? How large is the auditorium? Who selects the speakers' themes? Who else is to speak? What are they to speak about? Precisely how long am I to speak? Who speaks before I do and who follows?

If you want to hit the nail on the head ask such questions as these. No occasional address can succeed unless it fits the occasion to a T. Many prominent men have lost prestige because they were too careless or too busy or too self-confident to respect the occasion and the audience by learning the exact conditions under which they were to speak. Leaving too much to the moment is taking a long chance and generally means a less effective speech, if not a failure.

Suitability is the big thing in an occasional speech. Commemorative occasions, unveilings, commencements, dedications, eulogies, and all the train of special public gatherings, offer rare opportunities for the display of tact and good sense in handling occasion, theme, and audience. When to be dignified and when colloquial, when to soar and when to ramble arm in arm with your hearers, when to flame and when to soothe, when to instruct and when to amuse—in a word, the whole matter of APPROPRIATENESS must constantly be in mind lest you write your speech on water.

Finally, remember the beatitude: Blessed is the man that maketh short speeches, for he shall be invited to speak again.

POINTS TO REMEMBER

1. The hidden value of ordinary dinner party speeches should not be underestimated.
2. The first essential step of occasional speaking is to observe the atmosphere.
3. Avoid long monologues at special occasions.

15

A SURE WAY OF MAKING ENEMIES—AND HOW TO AVOID IT

You can tell people they are wrong by a look or an intonation or a gesture just as eloquently as you can in words—and if you tell them they are wrong, do you make them want to agree with you? Never! For you have struck a direct blow at their intelligence, judgment, pride, and self-respect. That will make them want to strike back. But it will never make them want to change their minds. You may then hurl at them all the logic of a Plato or an Immanuel Kant, but you will not alter their opinions, for you have hurt their feelings.

Never begin by announcing, "I am going to prove so-and-so to you." That's bad. That's tantamount to saying: "I'm smarter than you are. I'm going to tell you a thing or two and make you change your mind."

That is a challenge. It arouses opposition and makes the listener want to battle with you before you even start. It is difficult, under even the most benign conditions, to change people's minds. So why make it harder? Why handicap yourself?

Well, I can't hope to be any smarter than Socrates, so I have quit telling people they are wrong. And I find that it pays.

If a person makes a statement that you think is wrong—yes,

even that you know is wrong—isn't it better to begin by saying: "Well, now, look. I thought otherwise, but I may be wrong. I frequently am. And if I am wrong, I want to be put right. Let's examine the facts."

There's magic, positive magic, in such phrases as: "I may be wrong. I frequently am. Let's examine the facts."

Nobody in the heavens above or on the earth will ever object to your saying: "I may be wrong. Let's examine the facts."

One of our class members who used this approach in dealing with customers was Harold Reinke, a Dodge dealer in Billings, Montana. He reported that because of the pressures of the automobile business, he was often hard-boiled and callous when dealing with customers complaints. This caused flared tempers, loss of business, and general unpleasantness.

He told his class: "Recognizing that this was getting me nowhere fast, I tried a new tack. I would say something like this: 'Our dealership has made so many mistakes that I am frequently ashamed. We have erred in your case. Tell me about it.'

"This approach becomes quite disarming, and by the time the customer releases his feelings, he is usually much more reasonable when it comes to settling the matter. In fact, several customers have thanked me for having such an understanding attitude. And two of them have even brought in friends to buy new cars. In this highly competitive market, we need more of this type of customer, and I believe that showing respect for all customers opinions and treating them diplomatically and courteously will help beat the competition."

You will never get into trouble by admitting that you may be wrong. That will stop all argument and inspire your opponent to be just as fair and open and broad-minded as you are. It will make him want to admit that he, too, may be wrong.

If you know positively that a person is wrong, and you

bluntly tell him or her so, what happens? Let me illustrate. Mr. S, a young New York attorney, once argued a rather important case before the United States Supreme Court *(Lustgarten v. Fleet Corporation 280 U.S. 320).* The case involved a considerable sum of money and an important question of law. During the argument, one of the Supreme Court justices said to him: "The statute of limitations is six years, is it not?"

Mr. S stopped, stared at the justice for a moment, and then said bluntly, "Your Honor, there is no statute of limitations in admiralty."

"A hush fell on the court," said Mr. S, as he related his experience to one of my classes, "and the temperature in the room seemed to drop to zero. I was right. Justice was wrong. And I had told him so. But did that make him friendly? No. I still believe that I had the law on my side. And I know that I spoke better than I ever spoke before. But I didn't persuade. I made the enormous blunder of telling a very learned and famous man that he was wrong."

Few people are logical. Most of us are prejudiced and biased. Most of us are blighted with preconceived notions, with jealousy, suspicion, fear, envy, and pride. And most citizens don't want to change their minds about their religion or their haircut or communism or their favorite movie star.

DIPLOMACY WILL TAKE YOU PLACES

If you want some excellent suggestions about dealing with people and managing yourself and improving your personality, read Benjamin Franklin's autobiography—one of the most fascinating life stories ever written, one of the classics of American literature. Ben Franklin tells how he conquered the iniquitous habit of argument and transformed himself into one of the most able, suave, and diplomatic men in American history.

One day, when Ben Franklin was a blundering youth, an old Quaker friend took him aside and lashed him with a few stinging truths, something like this:

> Ben, you are impossible. Your opinions have a slap in them for everyone who differs with you. They have become so offensive that nobody cares for them. Your friends find they enjoy themselves better when you are not around. You know so much that no man can tell you anything. Indeed, no man is going to try, for the effort would lead only to discomfort and hard work. So you are not likely ever to know any more than you do now, which is very little.

One of the finest things I know about Ben Franklin is the way he accepted that smarting rebuke. He was big enough and wise enough to realize that it was true, to sense that he was headed for failure and social disaster. So he made a right-about-face. He began immediately to change his insolent, opinionated ways.

"I made it a rule," said Franklin, "to forbear all direct contradiction to the sentiment of others, and all positive assertion of my own. I even forbade myself the use of every word or expression in the language that imported a fix'd opinion, such as 'certainly,' 'undoubtedly,' etc., and I adopted, instead of them, 'I conceive,' 'I apprehend,' or 'I imagine' a thing to be so or so, or 'it so appears to me at present.' When another asserted something that I thought an error, I deny'd myself the pleasure of contradicting him abruptly, and of showing immediately some absurdity in his proposition: and in answering I began by observing that in certain cases or instances his opinion would be right, but in the present case there appear'd or seem'd to me some difference, etc. I soon found the advantage of this change in my manner; the conversations I engag'd in went on more pleasantly. The modest way in which I propos'd my opinions procur'd them a readier reception and less contradiction; I had less mortification when I was found to be in the wrong, and I more easily prevail'd with others to give up their mistakes and join with me when I happened to be in the right.

"And this mode, which I at first put on with some violence to natural inclination, became at length so easy, and so habitual to me, that perhaps for these fifty years past no one has ever heard a dogmatical expression escape me. And to this habit (after my character of integrity) I think it principally owing that I had earned so much weight with my fellow citizens when I proposed new institutions, or alterations in the old, and so much influence in public councils when I became a member; for I was but a bad speaker, never eloquent, subject to much hesitation in my choice of words, hardly correct in language, and yet I generally carried my points."

How do Ben Franklin's methods work in business? Let's take two examples.

Katherine A. Allred of Kings Mountain, North Carolina, is an industrial engineering supervisor for a yarn-processing plant. She told one of our classes how she handled a sensitive problem before and after taking our training:

"Part of my responsibility," she reported, "deals with setting up and maintaining incentive systems and standards for our operators so they can make more money by producing more yarn. The system we were using had worked fine when we had only two or three different types of yarn, but recently we had expanded our inventory and capabilities to enable us to run more than twelve different varieties. The present system was no longer adequate to pay the operators fairly for the work being performed and give them an incentive to increase production.

I had worked up a new system which would enable us to pay the operator by the class of yarn she was running at any one particular time. With my new system in hand, I entered the meeting determined to prove to the management that my system was the right approach. I told them in detail how they were wrong and showed where they were being unfair and how I had all the answers they needed. To say the least, I failed miserably! I had become so busy defending my position on the new system that I had left them no opening to graciously admit their problems on the old one. The issue was dead.

"After several sessions of this course, I realized all too well where I had made my mistakes. I called another meeting and this time I asked where they felt their problems were. We discussed each point, and I asked them their opinions on which was the best way to proceed. With a few low-keyed suggestions, at proper intervals, I let them develop my system themselves. At the end of the meeting when I actually presented my system, they enthusiastically accepted it.

"I am convinced now that nothing good is accomplished and a lot of damage can be done if you tell a person straight out that he or she is wrong. You only succeed in stripping that person of self-dignity and making yourself an unwelcome part of any discussion."

Let's take another example—and remember these cases I am citing are typical of the experiences of thousands of other people. R. V. Crowley was a salesman for a lumber company in New York. Crowley admitted that he had been telling hard-boiled lumber inspectors for years that they were wrong. And he had won the arguments too. But it hadn't done any good. "For these lumber inspectors," said Mr. Crowley, "are like baseball umpires. Once they make a decision, they never change it."

Mr. Crowley saw that his firm was losing thousands of

dollars through the arguments he won. So while taking my course, he resolved to change tactics and abandon arguments. With what results? Here is the story as he told it to the fellow members of his class:

"One morning the phone rang in my office. A hot and bothered person at the other end proceeded to inform me that a car of lumber we had shipped into his plant was entirely unsatisfactory. His firm had stopped unloading and requested that we make immediate arrangements to remove the stock from their yard. After about one-fourth of the car had been unloaded, their lumber inspector reported that the lumber was running fifty-five percent below grade. Under the circumstances, they refused to accept it.

"I immediately started for his plant and on the way turned over in my mind the best way to handle the situation. Ordinarily, under such circumstances, I should have quoted grading rules and tried, as a result of my own experience and knowledge as a lumber inspector, to convince the other inspector that the lumber was actually up to grade, and that he was misinterpreting the rules in his inspection. However, I thought I would apply the principles learned in this training.

"When I arrived at the plant, I found the purchasing agent and the lumber inspector in a wicked humor, both set for an argument and a fight. We walked out to the car that was being unloaded, and I requested that they continue to unload so that I could see how things were going. I asked the inspector to go right ahead and lay out the rejects, as he had been doing, and to put the good pieces in another pile.

"After watching him for a while it began to dawn on me that his inspection actually was much too strict and that he was misinterpreting the rules. This particular lumber was white pine, and I knew the inspector was thoroughly schooled in hard woods but not a competent, experienced inspector on white pine. White pine happened to be my own strong suit, but did I offer any objection to the way he was grading the lumber? None whatever. I kept on watching and gradually began to ask questions as to why certain pieces were not satisfactory. I didn't for one instant insinuate that the inspector was wrong. I emphasized that my only reason for asking was in order that we could give his firm exactly what they wanted in future shipments.

"By asking questions in a very friendly, cooperative spirit, and insisting continually that they were right in laying out boards not satisfactory to their purpose, I got him warmed up, and the strained relations between us began to thaw and melt away. An occasional carefully put remark on my part gave birth to the idea in his mind that possibly some of these rejected pieces were actually within the grade that they had bought, and that their requirements demanded a more expensive grade. I was very careful, however, not to let him think I was making an issue of this point.

"Gradually his whole attitude changed. He finally admitted to me that he was not experienced on white pine and began to ask me questions about each piece as it came out of the car. I would explain why such a piece came within the grade specified, but kept on insisting that we did not want him to take it if it was unsuitable for their purpose. He finally got to the point where he felt guilty every time he put a piece in he rejected pile. And at last he saw that the mistake was on their part for not having specified as good a grade as they needed.

"The ultimate outcome was that he went through the entire carload again after I left, accepted the whole lot, and we received a check in full.

"In that one instance alone, a little tact, and the determination to refrain from telling the other man he was wrong, saved my company a substantial amount of cash, and it would be hard to place a money value on the good will that was saved."

Martin Luther King, Jr., was asked how, as a pacifist, he could be an admirer of Air Force General Daniel "Chappie" James, then the nation's highest-ranking black officer. Dr. King replied, "I judge people by their own principles—not by my own."

In a similar way, General Robert E. Lee once spoke to the president of the Confederacy, Jefferson Davis in the most glowing terms about a certain officer under his command. Another officer was astonished. "General," he said, "do you not know that the man of whom you speak so highly is one of your bitterest enemies who misses no opportunity to malign you?" "Yes," replied General Lee, "but the president asked my opinion of him; he did not ask for his opinion of me."

By the way, I am not revealing anything new in this chapter. Two thousand years ago, Jesus said: "Agree with thine adversary quickly."

And twenty-two hundred years before Christ was born, Pharaoh Akhtoi of Egypt gave his son some shrewd advice—advice that is sorely needed today. "Be diplomatic," counseled the pharaoh. "It will help you gain your point."

In other words, don't argue with your customer or your spouse or your adversary. Don't tell them they are wrong, don't get them stirred up. Use a little diplomacy.

POINTS TO REMEMBER

1. Quit telling people they are wrong.
2. Admit you are at fault and you'll never get into trouble.
3. Be Switzerland.

16

A MAGIC FORMULA

Would you like a quick, sure-fire recipe for handling worry situations—a technique you can start using right away, before you go any further in reading this book?

Then let me tell you about the method worked out by Willis H. Carrier, the brilliant engineer who launched the air-conditioning industry, and who is now head of the world-famous Carrier Corporation, in Syracuse, New York. It is one of the best techniques I ever heard of for solving worry problems, and I got it from Mr. Carrier personally when we were having lunch together one day at the Engineers' Club in New York.

"When I was a young man," Mr. Carrier said, "I worked for the Buffalo Forge Company in Buffalo, New York. I was handed the assignment of installing a gas-cleaning device in a plant of the Pittsburgh Plate Glass Company at Crystal City, Missouri—a plant costing millions of dollars. The purpose of this installation was to remove the impurities from the gas so it could be burned without injuring the engines. This method of cleaning gas was new. It had been tried only once before—and under different conditions. In my work at Crystal City, Missouri, unforeseen difficulties arose. It worked after a fashion—but not well enough to meet the guarantee we had made.

"I was stunned by my failure. It was almost as if someone

had struck me a blow on the head. My stomach, my insides, began to twist and turn. For a while I was so worried I couldn't sleep.

"Finally, common sense reminded me that worry wasn't getting me anywhere; so I figured out a way to handle my problem without worrying. It worked superbly. I have been using this same anti-worry technique for more than thirty years. It is simple. Anyone can use it. It consists of three steps:

"Step I. *I analyzed the situation fearlessly and honestly and figured out what was the worst that could possibly happen as a result of this failure.* No one was going to jail me or shoot me. That was certain. True, there was a chance that I would lose my position; and there was also a chance that my employers would have to remove the machinery and lose the twenty thousand dollars we had invested.

"Step II. *After figuring out what was the worst that could possibly happen, I reconciled myself to accepting it, if necessary.* I said to myself: This failure will be a blow to my record, and it might possibly mean the loss of my job; but if it does, I can always get another position. Conditions could be much worse; and as far as my employers are concerned—well, they realize that we are experimenting with a new method of cleaning gas, and if this experience costs them twenty thousand dollars, they can stand it. They can charge it up to research, for it is an experiment.

"After discovering the worst that could possibly happen and reconciling myself to accepting it, if necessary, an extremely important thing happened: I immediately relaxed and felt a sense of peace that I hadn't experienced in days.

"Step III. *From that time on, I calmly devoted my time and energy to trying to improve upon the worst which I had already accepted mentally.*

"I now tried to figure out ways and means by which I might reduce the loss of twenty thousand dollars that we faced. I made several tests and finally figured out that if we spent another five thousand for additional equipment, our problem would be solved. We did this, and instead of the firm losing twenty thousand, we made fifteen thousand.

"I probably would never have been able to do this if I had kept on worrying, because one of the worst features about worrying is that it destroys our ability to concentrate. When we worry, our minds jump here and there and everywhere, and we lose all power of decision. However, when we force ourselves to face the worst and accept it mentally, we then eliminate all these vague imaginings and put ourselves in a position in which we are able to concentrate on our problem.

"This incident that I have related occurred many years ago. It worked so superbly that I have been using it ever since; and, as a result, my life has been almost completely free from worry."

Now, why is Willis H. Carrier's magic formula so valuable and so practical, psychologically speaking? Because it yanks us down out of the great gray clouds in which we fumble around when we are blinded by worry. It plants our feet good and solid on the earth. We know where we stand. And if we haven't solid ground under us, how in creation can we ever hope to think anything through?

The same idea was expressed by Lin Yutang in his widely read book, *The Importance of Living.* "True peace of mind," said this Chinese philosopher, "comes from accepting the worst. Psychologically, I think, it means a release of energy."

That's it, exactly! Psychologically, it means a new release of energy! When we have accepted the worst, we have nothing more to lose. And that automatically means—we have *everything* to gain! "After facing the worst," Willis H. Carrier reported,

"I immediately relaxed and felt a sense of peace that I hadn't experienced in days. From that time on, I was able to *think.*"

Makes sense, doesn't it? Yet millions of people have wrecked their lives in angry turmoil, because they refused to accept the worst; refused to try to improve upon it; refused to salvage what they could from the wreck. Instead of trying to reconstruct their fortunes, they engaged in a bitter and "violent contest with experience"—and ended up victims of that brooding fixation known as melancholia.

Would you like to see how someone else adopted Willis H. Carrier's magic formula and applied it to his own problem? Well, here is one example, from a New York oil dealer who was a student in my classes.

"I was being blackmailed!" this student began. "I didn't believe it was possible—I didn't believe it could happen outside of the movies—but I was actually being blackmailed! What happened was this: the oil company of which I was the head had a number of delivery trucks and a number of drivers. At that time, OPA regulations were strictly in force, and we were rationed on the amount of oil we could deliver to any one of our customers. I didn't know it, but it seems that certain of our drivers had been delivering oil short to our regular customers, and then reselling the surplus to customers of their own.

"The first inkling I had of these illegitimate transactions was when a man who claimed to be a government inspector came to see me one day and demanded hush money. He had got documentary proof of what our drivers had been doing, and he threatened to turn this proof over to the District Attorney's office if I didn't cough up.

"I knew, of course, that I had nothing to worry about—personally, at least. But I also knew that the law says a firm is responsible for the actions of its employees. What's more, I knew that if the case came to court, and it was aired in the newspapers, the bad publicity would ruin my business. And I was proud of my business—it had been founded by my father twenty-four years before.

"I was so worried I was sick! I didn't eat or sleep for three days and nights. I kept going around in crazy circles. Should I pay the money—five thousand dollars—or should I tell this man to go ahead and do his damnedest? Either way I tried to make up my mind, it ended in nightmare.

"Then, on Sunday night, I happened to pick up the booklet on *How to Stop Worrying* which I had been given in my Carnegie class in public speaking. I started to read it, and came across the story of Willis H. Carrier. 'Face the worst,' it said. So I asked myself, 'What is the worst that can happen if I refuse to pay up, and these blackmailers turn their records over to the District Attorney?'

"The answer to that was: 'The ruin of my business—that's the worst that can happen. I can't go to jail. All that can happen is that I shall be ruined by the publicity.'

"I then said to myself, 'All right, the business *is* ruined. I accept that mentally. What happens next?'

"Well, with my business ruined, I would probably have to look for a job. That wasn't bad. I knew a lot about oil—there were several firms that might be glad to employ me... I began to feel better. The blue funk I had been in for three days and nights began to lift a little. My emotions calmed down... And to my astonishment, I was able to *think*.

"I was clearheaded enough now to face Step III—*improve on the worst*. As I thought of solutions, an entirely new angle presented itself to me. If I told my attorney the whole situation, he might find a way out which I hadn't thought of. I know it sounds stupid to say that this hadn't even occurred to me before—but of course I hadn't been thinking, I had only been *worrying!* I immediately made up my mind that I would see my attorney first thing in the morning—and then I went to bed and slept like a log!

"How did it end? Well, the next morning my lawyer told me to go and see the District Attorney and tell him the truth. I did precisely that. When I finished I was astonished to hear the D.A. say that this blackmail racket had been going on for months and that the man who claimed to be a 'government agent' was a crook wanted by the police. What a relief to hear all this after I tormented myself for three days and nights wondering whether I should hand over five thousand dollars to this professional swindler!

"This experience taught me a lasting lesson. Now, whenever I face a pressing problem that threatens to worry me, I give it what I call 'the old Willis H. Carrier formula.'"

If you think Willis H. Carrier had troubles—listen: you ain't heard nothin' yet.

PAUSE AND RELAX, IT MIGHT SAVE YOUR LIFE

Here is the story of Earl P. Haney, who lives at 52 Wedgemere Avenue, Winchester, Massachusetts. Here is the story as he told it to me himself on November 17, 1948, in the Hotel Statler in Boston.

"Back in the twenties," he said, "I was so worried that ulcers began eating the lining of my stomach. One night, I had a terrible hemorrhage. I was rushed to a hospital connected with the School of Medicine of Northwestern University in Chicago. My weight dropped from 175 pounds to 90 pounds. I was so ill I was warned not even to lift my hand. Three doctors, including a celebrated ulcer specialist, said my case was 'incurable.' I lived on alkaline powders and a tablespoonful of half milk and half cream every hour. A nurse put a rubber tube down into my stomach every night and morning and pumped out the contents.

"This went on for months... Finally, I said to myself: 'Look here, Earl Haney, if you have nothing to look forward to except a lingering death, you might as well make the most of the little time you have left. You have always wanted to travel around the world before you die; so if you are ever going to do it, you'll have to do it now.'

"When I told my physicians I was going to travel around the world and pump out my own stomach twice a day, they were shocked. Impossible! They had never heard of such a thing. They warned me that if I started around the world, I would be buried at sea. 'No, I won't,' I replied. 'I have promised my relatives that I will be buried in the family plot at Broken Bow, Nebraska. So I am going to take my casket with me.'

"I arranged for a casket, put it aboard ship, and then made arrangements with the steamship company—in the event of my death—to put my corpse in a freezing compartment and keep it there till the liner returned home. I set out on my trip, imbued with the spirit of old Omar:

> Ah, make the most of what we yet may spend,
> Before we too into the Dust descend;
> Dust into Dust, and under Dust, to lie,
> Sans Wine, sans Song, sans Singer, and—sans End!

"The moment I boarded the *S.S. President Adams* in Los Angeles and headed for the Orient, I felt better. I gradually gave up my alkaline powders and my stomach pump. I was soon eating all kinds of foods—even strange native mixtures and concoctions that were guaranteed to kill me. As the weeks went by, I even smoked long, black cigars and drank highballs. I enjoyed myself more than I had in years! We ran into monsoons and typhoons which should have put me in my casket, if only from fright—but I got an enormous kick out of all this adventure.

"I played games aboard the ship, sang songs, made new friends, stayed up half the night. When we reached China and India, I realized that the business cares that I had faced back home were paradise compared to the poverty and hunger in the Orient. I stopped all my senseless worrying and felt fine. When I got back to America, I had gained ninety pounds and I had almost forgotten had ever had a stomach ulcer. I had never felt better in my life. I went back to business and haven't been ill a day since."

Earl P. Haney told me he realizes now that he was unconsciously using the selfsame principles that Willis H. Carrier used to conquer worry.

"First, I asked myself, 'What is the worst that could possibly happen?' The answer was death.

"Second, I prepared myself to accept death. I had to. There was no choice. The doctors said my case was hopeless.

"Third, I tried to improve the situation by getting the utmost enjoyment out of life for the short time I had left. ... If," he continued, "if I had gone on worrying after boarding that ship, I have no doubt that I would have made the return voyage inside my coffin. But I relaxed—and I forgot all my troubles. And this calmness of mind gave me a new birth of energy which actually saved my life."

So, Rule 2 is: If you have a worry problem, apply the magic formula of Willis H. Carrier by doing these three things:

Ask yourself, "What is the worst that can possibly happen?"

Prepare to accept it if you have to.

Then calmly proceed to improve on the worst.

You're only here for a short visit. Don't hurry, don't worry.
And be sure to smell the flowers along the way.
—Walter Hagen

POINTS TO REMEMBER

1. Follow the anti-worry technique to cope with failure.
2. Accept the worst possible outcome and nothing can stop you.
3. Enjoying life is essential to remain motivated.

17

THE TALK TO CONVINCE

There was once a small group of men and women who found themselves in the path of a hurricane. Not a real hurricane, but the next thing to it. In short, a hurricane of a man named Maurice Goldblatt. Here is how one of that group described it:

> We were sitting around a luncheon table in Chicago. We knew this man was reputed to be a powerful speaker. We watched him intently as he stood up to speak.
>
> He began quietly—a spruce, pleasant man of middle age—thanking us for inviting him. He wanted to talk about something serious, he said, and he hoped we would forgive him if he disturbed us.
>
> Then, like a whirlwind, he struck. He leaned forward and his eyes transfixed us. He didn't raise his voice, but it seemed to me that it crashed like a gong.
>
> "Look around you," he said. "Look at one another. Do you know how many of you sitting now in this room are going to die of cancer? One in four of all of you who are over forty-five. One in four!"
>
> He paused, and his face lightened. "That's a plain, harsh fact, but it needn't be for long," he said. "Something

can be done about it. This something is progress in the treatment of cancer and in the search for its cause."

He looked at us gravely, his gaze moving around the table. "Do you want to help toward this progress?" he asked.

Could there have been an answer except "Yes!" in the minds of any of us then? "Yes!" I thought, and I found later that so did the others.

In less than a minute, Maurice Goldblatt had won us. He had drawn us personally into his subject. He had us on his side, in the campaign he was waging for a humanitarian cause.

Getting a favorable reaction is every speaker's objective any time, anywhere. As it happened, Mr. Goldblatt had a dramatically good reason for wanting to get one from us. He and his brother, Nathan, starting with little more than nothing, had built up a department store chain doing a business of more than $100,000,000 a year. Fabulous success had come to them after long, hard years, and then Nathan, ill only a short time, had died of cancer. After that, Maurice Goldblatt saw to it that the Goldblatt Foundation gave the first million dollars to the University of Chicago's cancer research program, and he gave his own time—retiring from business—to the work of interesting the public in the fight against cancer.

These facts, together with Maurice Goldblatt's personality, won us. Sincerity, earnestness, enthusiasm—a blazing determination to give himself to us for a few minutes, just as he was giving himself year in and out to a great cause—all of these factors swept us up into a feeling of agreement with the speaker, a friendliness for him, a willingness to be interested and moved.

FIRST: WIN CONFIDENCE BY DESERVING IT

Quintilian described the orator as "a good man skilled in speaking." He was talking about sincerity and character. Nothing said in this book, nor anything which will be said, can take the place of this essential attribute of speaking effectiveness. Pierpont Morgan said that character was the best way to obtain credit; it is also the best way to win the confidence of the audience.

"The sincerity with which a man speaks," said Alexander Woolcott, "imparts to his voice a color of truth no perjurer can feign."

Especially when the purpose of our talk is to convince, it is necessary to set forth our own ideas with the inner glow that comes from sincere conviction. We must first be convinced before we attempt to convince others.

SECOND: GET A YES-RESPONSE

Walter Dill Scott, former president of Northwestern University, said that "every idea, concept, or conclusion which enters the mind is held as true unless hindered by some contradictory idea." That boils down to keeping the audience yes-minded. My good friend Professor Harry Overstreet brilliantly examined the psychological background of this concept in a lecture at the New School for Social Research in New York City:

> The skillful speaker gets at the outset a number of yes-responses. He has thereby set the psychological processes of his listeners moving in the affirmative direction. It is like the movement of a billiard ball. Propel it in one direction, and it takes some force to deflect it, far more force to send it back in the opposite direction.

> The psychological patterns here are quite clear.
>
> When a person says "No" and really means it, he is doing far more than saying a word of two letters. His entire organism—glandular, nervous, muscular—gathers itself together into a condition of rejection. There is, usually in minute but sometimes in observable degree, a physical withdrawal, or readiness for withdrawal. The whole neuromuscular system, in short, sets itself on guard against acceptance. Where, on the contrary, a person says "Yes," none of the withdrawing activities takes place. The organism is in a forward-moving, accepting, open attitude. Hence the more "Yesses" we can, at the very outset, induce, the more likely we are to succeed in capturing the attention for our ultimate proposal.
>
> It is a very simple technique—this yes-response. And yet how much neglected! It often seems as if people get a sense of their own importance by antagonizing at the outset. The radical comes into a conference with his conservative brethren; and immediately he must make them furious! What, as a matter of fact, is the good of it? If he simply does it in order to get some pleasure out of it for himself, he may be pardoned. But if he expects to achieve something, he is only psychologically stupid.
>
> Get a student to say "No" at the beginning, or a customer, child, husband, or wife, and it takes the wisdom and patience of angels to transform that bristling negative into an affirmative.

How is one going to get these desirable "yes-responses" at the very outset? Fairly simple. "My way of opening and winning an argument," confided Lincoln, "is to first find a common ground of agreement." Lincoln found it even when he was discussing the highly inflammable subject of slavery. "For the first half hour," declared *The Mirror*, a neutral paper reporting one of his talks, "his opponents would agree with every word he uttered. From that point he began to lead them off, little by little, until it seemed as if he had got them all into his fold."

Is it not evident that the speaker who argues with his audience is merely arousing their stubbornness, putting them on the defensive, making it well-nigh impossible for them to change their minds? Is it wise to start by saying, "I am going to prove so and so"? Aren't your hearers liable to accept that as a challenge and remark silently, "Let's see you do it"?

Is it not much more advantageous to begin by stressing something that you and all of your hearers believe, and then to raise some pertinent question that everyone would like to have answered? Then take your audience with you in an earnest search for the answer. While on that search, present the facts as you see them so clearly that they will be led to accept your conclusions as their own. They will have much more faith in some truth that they have discovered for themselves. "The best argument is that which seems merely an explanation."

In every controversy, no matter how wide and bitter the differences, there is always some common ground of agreement on which a speaker can invite everyone to meet. To illustrate: On February 3, 1960, the prime minister of Great Britain, Harold Macmillan, addressed both houses of the Parliament of the Union of South Africa. He had to present the United Kingdom's non-racial viewpoint before the legislature body at a time when apartheid was the prevailing policy. Did he begin his talk with this essential difference in outlook? No. He began by stressing the great economic progress made by South Africa, the significant contributions made by South Africa to the world. Then, with skill and tact he brought up the questions of differing viewpoints. Even here, he indicated that he was well aware that these differences were based on sincere conviction. His whole talk was a masterly statement reminding one of Lincoln's gentle but firm utterances in the years before Fort Sumter. "As a fellow member of the Commonwealth," said the Prime Minister, "it is our earnest desire to give South Africa our support and encouragement, but I hope you won't mind my saying frankly that there are some aspects of your policies which make it impossible for us to do this without being false to our deep convictions about the political destinies of free men to which in our own territories we are trying to give effect. I think we ought as friends to face together, without seeking to apportion credit or blame, the fact that in the world of today this difference of outlook lies between us."

No matter how determined one was to differ with a speaker, a statement like that would tend to convince you of the speaker's fair-mindedness.

What would have been the result had Prime Minister Macmillan set out immediately to emphasize the difference in policy rather than the common ground of agreement? Professor James Harvey Robinson's enlightening book, *The Mind in the Making,* gives the psychological answer to that question:

> We sometimes find ourselves changing our minds without any resistance or heavy emotion, but if we are told we are wrong we resent the imputation and harden our hearts. We are incredibly heedless in the formation of our beliefs, but find ourselves filled with an illicit passion for them when anyone proposes to rob us of their companionship. It is obviously not the ideas themselves that are dear to us, but our self-esteem which is threatened... The little word *my* is the most important

> one in human affairs, and properly to reckon with it is the beginning of wisdom. It has the same force whether it is *my* dinner, *my* dog, and *my* house, or *my* faith, *my* country and *my* God. We not only resent the imputation that our watch is wrong, or our car shabby, but that our conception of the canals of Mars, of the pronunciation of "Epictetus," of the medicinal value of salicine, or of the date of Sargon I, are subject to revision... We like to continue to believe what we have been accustomed to accept as true, and the resentment aroused when doubt is cast upon any of our assumptions leads us to seek every manner of excuse for clinging to it. The result is that most of our so-called reasoning consists in finding arguments for going on believing as we already do.

THIRD: SPEAK WITH CONTAGIOUS ENTHUSIASM

Contradicting ideas are much less likely to arise in the listener's mind when the speaker presents his ideas with feeling and contagious enthusiasm. I say "contagious," for enthusiasm is just that. It thrusts aside all negative and opposing ideas. When your aim is to convince, remember it is more productive to stir emotions than to arouse thoughts. Feelings are more powerful than cold ideas. To arouse feelings one must be intensely in earnest. Regardless of the petty phrases a man may concoct, regardless of the illustrations he may assemble, regardless of the harmony of his voice and the grace of his gestures, if he does not speak sincerely, these are hollow and glittering trappings. If you would impress an audience, be impressed yourself. Your spirit, shining through your eyes, radiating through your voice, and proclaiming itself through your manner, will communicate itself to your audience.

Every time you speak, and especially when your avowed purpose is to convince, what you do determines the attitude of your listeners. If you are lukewarm, so will they be; if you are flippant and antagonistic, so will they be. "When the congregation falls asleep," wrote Henry Ward Beecher, "there is only one thing to do; provide the usher with a sharp stick and have him prod the preacher."

I was once one of three judges called on to award the Curtis medal at Columbia University. There were half a dozen undergraduates, all of them elaborately trained, all of them eager to acquit themselves well. But—with only a single exception—what they were striving for was to win the medal. They had little or no desire to convince.

They had chosen their topics because these topics permitted oratorical development. They had no deep personal interest in the arguments they were making. And their successive talks were merely exercises in the art of delivery.

The exception was a Zulu Prince. He had selected as his theme "The Contribution of Africa to Modern Civilization." He put intense feeling into every word he uttered. His talk was no mere exercise; it was a living thing, born of conviction and enthusiasm. He spoke as the representative of his people, of his continent; with wisdom, high character, and good will, he brought us a message of his people's hopes and a plea for our understanding.

We gave him the medal although he was possibly no more accomplished in addressing a large group than two or three of his competitors. What we judges recognized was that his talk had the true fire of sincerity; it was ablaze with truth. Beside it, the other talks were only flickering gas-logs.

The Prince had learned in his own way in a distant land that you can't project your personality in a talk to others by using reason alone: you have to reveal to them how deeply you yourself believe in what you say.

FOURTH: SHOW RESPECT AND AFFECTION FOR YOUR AUDIENCE

"The human personality demands love and it also demands respect," Dr. Norman Vincent Peale said as a prelude to speaking of a professional comedian. "Every human being has an inner sense of worth, of importance, of dignity. Wound that and you have lost that person forever. So when you love and respect a person you build him up and, accordingly, he loves and esteems you.

"At one time I was on a program with an entertainer. I did not know the man well, but since that meeting I read that he was having difficulty, and I think I know why.

"I had been sitting beside him quietly for I was about to speak. 'You aren't nervous, are you?' he asked

"'Why, yes,' I replied. 'I always get a little nervous before I stand up before an audience. I have a profound respect for an audience and the responsibility makes me a bit nervous. Don't you get nervous?'

"'No,' he said, 'Why should I? Audiences fall for anything. They are a lot of dopes.'

"'I don't agree with you,' I said. They are your sovereign judges. I have great respect for audiences.'"

When he read about this man's waning popularity Dr. Peale was sure the reason lay in an attitude that antagonized others instead of winning them.

What an object lesson for all of us who want to impart something to other people!

FIFTH: BEGIN IN A FRIENDLY WAY

An atheist once challenged William Paley to disprove his contention that there was no Supreme Being. Very quietly Paley took out his watch, opened the case, and said: "If I were to tell you that those levers and wheels and springs made themselves and fitted themselves together and started running on their own account, wouldn't you question my intelligence? Of course, you would. But look up at the stars. Every one of them has its perfect appointed course and motion—the earth and planets around the sun, and the whole group pitching along at more than a million miles a day. Each star is another sun with its own group of worlds, rushing on through space like our own solar system. Yet there are no collisions, no disturbance, no confusion. All quiet, efficient, and controlled. Is it easier to believe that they just happened or that someone made them so?"

Suppose he had retorted to his antagonist at the outset: "No God? Don't be a silly ass. You don't know what you are talking about." What would have happened? Doubtlessly a verbal joust—a wordy war would have ensued, as futile as it was fiery. The atheist would have risen with an unholy zeal upon him to fight for his opinions with all the fury of a wildcat. Why? Because, as Professor Overstreet has pointed out, they were *his* opinions, and his precious, indispensable self-esteem would have been threatened; his pride would have been at stake.

Since pride is such a fundamentally explosive characteristic of human nature, wouldn't it be the part of wisdom to get a man's pride working for us, instead of against us? How? By showing, as Paley did, that the thing we propose is very similar to something that our opponent already believes. That renders it easier for him to accept than to reject your proposal. That prevents contradictory and opposing ideas from arising in the mind to vitiate what we have said.

Paley showed delicate appreciation of how the human mind functions. Most men, however, lack this subtle ability to enter the citadel of a man's beliefs arm in arm with the owner. They erroneously imagine that in order to take the citadel, they must storm it, batter it down by a frontal attack. What happens? The moment hostilities commence, the drawbridge is lifted, the great gates are slammed and bolted, the mailed archers draw their long bows—the battle of words and wounds is on. Such frays always end in a draw; neither has convinced the other of anything.

This more sensible method I am advocating is not new. It was used long ago by Saint Paul. He employed it in that famous address of his to the Athenians on Mars Hill—employed it with an adroitness and finesse that compels our admiration across nineteen centuries. He was a man of finished education; and, after his conversion to Christianity, his eloquence made him its leading advocate. One day he arrived at Athens—the post-Pericles Athens, an Athens that had passed the summit of its glory and was now on the decline. The Bible says of it at this period: "All the Athenians and strangers which were there spent their time in nothing else but either to tell or to hear some new thing."

No radios, no cables, no news dispatches; those Athenians must have been hard put in those days to scratch up something fresh every afternoon. Then Paul came. Here was something new. They crowded about him, amused, curious, interested. Taking him to the Aeropagus, they said: "May we know what this new doctrine, whereof thou speakest, is? For thou bringest certain strange things to our ears: we would know therefore what these things mean."

In other words, they invited a speech; and, nothing loath,

Paul agreed. In fact, that was what he had come for. He probably stood up on a block or stone, and, being a bit nervous, as all good speakers are at the very outset, he may have given his hands a dry wash, and have cleared his throat before he began.

However, he did not altogether approve of the way they had worded their invitation; "New doctrines…strange things." That was poison. He must eradicate those ideas. They were fertile ground for the propagating of contradictory and clashing opinions. He did not wish to present his faith as something strange and alien. He wanted to tie it up to, liken it to, something they already believed. That would smother dissenting suggestions. But how? He thought a moment; hit upon a brilliant plan; he began his immortal address: "Ye men of Athens, I perceive that in all things ye are very superstitious."

Some translations read, "Ye are very religious." I think that is better, more accurate. They worshipped many gods; they were very religious. They were proud of it. He complimented them, pleased them. They began to warm toward him. One of the rules of the art of effective speaking is to support a statement by an illustration. He does just that:

"For, as I passed by, and beheld your devotions, I found an altar with this inscription, TO THE UNKNOWN GOD."

That proves, you see, that they were very religious. They were so afraid of slighting one of the deities that they had put up an altar to the unknown God, a sort of blanket insurance policy to provide against all unconscious slights and unintentional oversights. Paul, by mentioning this specific altar, indicated that he was not dealing in flattery; he showed that his remark was a genuine appreciation born of observation.

Now, here comes the consummate rightness of this opening: "Whom therefore ye ignorantly worship, Him declare I unto you."

"New doctrine...strange things?" Not a bit of it. He was there merely to explain a few truths about a God they were already worshipping without being conscious of it. Likening the things they did not believe, you see, to something they already passionately accepted—such was his superb technique.

He pronounced his doctrine of salvation and resurrection, quoted a few words from one of their own Greek poets; and he was done. Some of his hearers mocked, but others said, "We will hear thee again on this matter."

Our problem in making a talk to convince or impress others is just this: to plant the idea in their minds and to keep contradicting and opposing ideas from arising. He who is skilled in doing that has power in speaking and influencing others. Here is precisely where the rules in my book *How to Win Friends and Influence People* will be helpful.

Almost every day of your life you are talking to people who differ from you on some subject under discussion. Aren't you constantly trying to win people to your way of thinking, at home, in the office, in social situations of all kinds? Is there room for improvement in your methods? How do you begin? By showing Lincoln's tact and Macmillan's? If so, you are a person of rare diplomacy and extraordinary discretion. It is well to remember Woodrow Wilson's words, "If you come to me and say, 'Let us sit down and take counsel together, and, if we differ from one another, understand why it is that we differ from one another, just what the points at issue are,' we will presently find that we are not so far apart after all, that the points on which we differ are few and the points on which we agree are many, and that if we only have the patience and the candor and the desire to get together, we will get together."

POINTS TO REMEMBER

1. The speech should reflect your sincerity.
2. Benefit from the 'Yes-Response' technique.
3. A friendly approach with the audience enables them to connect with you better.

18

VOICE CHARM

Poe said that "the tone of beauty is sadness," but he was evidently thinking from cause to effect, not contrariwise, for sadness is rarely a producer of beauty—that is peculiarly the province of joy.

The exquisite beauty of a sunset is not exhilarating but tends to a sort of melancholy that is not far from delight. The haunting beauty of deep, quiet music holds more than a tinge of sadness. The lovely minor cadences of bird song at twilight are almost depressing.

The reason we are affected to sadness by certain forms of placid beauty is twofold: Movement is stimulating and joy-producing, while quietude leads to reflection, and reflection in turn often brings out the tone of regretful longing for that which is past; secondly, quiet beauty produces a vague aspiration for the relatively unattainable, yet does not stimulate to the tremendous effort necessary to make the dimly desired state or object ours.

We must distinguish, for these reasons, between the sadness of beauty and the joy of beauty. True, joy is a deep, inner thing and takes in much more than the idea of bounding, sanguine spirits, for it includes a certain active contentedness of heart. In this chapter, however the word will have its optimistic, exuberant connotation—we are thinking now of vivid, bright-eyed, laughing joy.

Musical, joyous tones constitute voice charm, a subtle magnetism that is delightfully contagious. Now it might seem to the desultory reader that to take the lancet and cut into this alluring voice quality would be to dissect a butterfly wing and so destroy its charm. Yet how can we induce an effect if we are not certain as to the cause?

NASAL RESONANCE PRODUCES THE BELL-TONES OF THE VOICE

The tone passages of the nose must be kept entirely free for the bright tones of voice—and you must not confuse what is popularly and erroneously called a "nasal" tone with the true nasal quality, which is so well illustrated by the voice work of trained French singers and speakers.

To develop nasal resonance sing the following, dwelling as long as possible on the ng sounds. Pitch the voice in the nasal cavity. Practice both in high and low registers, and develop range—with brightness.

> Sing-song. Ding-dong. Hong-kong. Long-thong.

Practice in the falsetto voice develops a bright quality in the normal speaking-voice. Try the following, and any other selections you choose, in a falsetto voice. A man's falsetto voice is extremely high and womanish, so men should not practice in falsetto after the exercise becomes tiresome.

> She perfectly scorned the best of his clan, and declared the ninth of any man, a perfectly vulgar fraction.

The actress Mary Anderson asked the poet Longfellow what she could do to improve her voice. He replied, "Read aloud daily, joyous, lyric poetry."

The joyous tones are the bright tones. Develop them by exercise. Practice your voice exercises in an attitude of joy. Under the influence of pleasure the body expands, the tone passages open, the action of heart and lungs is accelerated, and all the primary conditions for good tone are established.

More songs float out from the broken windows of the negro cabins in the South than from the palatial homes on Fifth Avenue. Henry Ward Beecher said the happiest days of his life were not when he had become an international character, but when he was an unknown minister out in Lawrenceville, Ohio, sweeping his own church, and working as a carpenter to help pay the grocer. Happiness is largely an attitude of mind, of viewing life from the right angle. The optimistic attitude can be cultivated, and it will express itself in voice charm. A telephone company recently placarded this motto in their booths: "The Voice with the Smile Wins." It does. Try it.

Reading joyous prose, or lyric poetry, will help put smile and joy of soul into your voice. The following selections are excellent for practice.

REMEMBER that when you first practice these classics you are to give sole attention to two things: a joyous attitude of heart and body, and bright tones of voice. After these ends have been attained to your satisfaction, carefully review the principles of public speaking laid down in the preceding chapters and put them into practice as you read these passages again and again. It would be better to commit each selection to memory.

In joyous conversation there is an elastic touch, a delicate stroke, upon the central ideas, generally following a pause. This elastic touch adds vivacity to the voice. If you try repeatedly, it can be sensed by feeling the tongue strike the teeth. The entire absence of elastic touch in the voice can be observed in the thick tongue of the intoxicated man. Try to talk with the tongue lying still in the bottom of the mouth, and you will obtain largely the same effect. Vivacity of utterance is gained by using the tongue to strike off the emphatic idea with a decisive, elastic touch.

Deliver the following with decisive strokes on the emphatic ideas. Deliver it in a vivacious manner, noting the elastic touch-action of the tongue. A flexible, responsive tongue is absolutely essential to good voice work.

From Napoleon's address to the directory on his return from Egypt:

> What have you done with that brilliant France which I left you? I left you at peace, and I find you at war. I left you victorious and I find you defeated. I left you the millions of Italy, and I find only spoliation and poverty. What have you done with the hundred thousand Frenchmen, my companions in glory? They are dead!... This state of affairs cannot last long; in less than three years it would plunge us into despotism.

The children at play on the street, glad from sheer physical vitality, display a resonance and charm in their voices quite different from the voices that float through the silent halls of the hospitals. A skilled physician can tell much about his patient's condition from the mere sound of the voice. Failing health, or even physical weariness, tells through the voice. It is always well to rest and be entirely refreshed before attempting to deliver a public address. As to health, neither scope nor space permits us to discuss here the laws of hygiene. There are many excellent books on this subject. In the reign of the Roman emperor

Tiberius, one senator wrote to another: "To the wise, a word is sufficient."

"The apparel oft proclaims the man;" the voice always does—it is one of the greatest revealers of character. The superficial woman, the brutish man, the reprobate, the person of culture, often discloses inner nature in the voice, for even the cleverest dissembler cannot entirely prevent its tones and qualities being affected by the slightest change of thought or emotion. In anger it becomes high, harsh, and unpleasant; in love low, soft, and melodious—the variations are as limitless as they are fascinating to observe. Visit a theatrical hotel in a large city, and listen to the buzz-saw voices of the chorus girls from some burlesque "attraction." The explanation is simple—buzz-saw lives. Emerson said: "When a man lives with God his voice shall be as sweet as the murmur of the brook or the rustle of the corn." It is impossible to think selfish thoughts and have either an attractive personality, a lovely character, or a charming voice. If you want to possess voice charm, cultivate a deep, sincere sympathy for mankind. Love will shine out through your eyes and proclaim itself in your tones. One secret of the sweetness of the canary's song may be his freedom from tainted thoughts. Your character beautifies or mars your voice. As a man thinketh in his heart, so is his voice.

POINTS TO REMEMBER

1. A joyful tone of voice is charming and charismatic.
2. Develop vocal range and nasal resonance for brightness in your intonation.
3. Practice the given passage and phrases with a focus on emphatic and vivacious delivery.

19

PUT A "STOP-LOSS" ORDER ON YOUR WORRIES

Would you like to know how to make money in Wall Street? Well, so would a million other people—and if I knew the answer, this book would sell for ten thousand dollars a copy. However, there's one good idea that some successful operators use. This story was told to me by Charles Roberts, an investment counselor with offices at 17 East 42nd Street, New York.

"I originally came to New York from Texas with twenty thousand dollars which my friends had given me to invest in the stock market," Charles Roberts told me. "I thought," he continued, "that I knew the ropes in the stock market; but I lost every cent. True, I made a lot of profit on some deals; but I ended up by losing everything.

"I did not mind so much losing my own money," Mr. Roberts explained, "but I felt terrible about having lost my friends' money, even though they could well afford it. I dreaded facing them again after our venture had turned out so unfortunately, but, to my astonishment, they not only were good sports about it, but proved to be incurable optimists.

"I knew I had been trading on a hit-or-miss basis and

depending largely on luck and other people's opinions. As H. I. Phillips said, I had been 'playing the stock market by ear.'

"I began to think over my mistakes and I was determined that before I went back into the market again, I would try to find out what it was all about. So I sought out and became acquainted with one of the most successful speculators who ever lived: Burton S. Castles. I believed I could learn a great deal from him because he had long enjoyed the reputation of being successful year after year and I knew that such a career was not the result of mere chance or luck.

"He asked me a few questions about how I had traded before and then told me what I believe is the most important principle in trading. He said, 'I put a stop-loss order on every market commitment I make. If I buy a stock at, say, fifty dollars a share, I immediately place a stop-loss order on it at forty-five.' That means that when and if the stock should decline as much as five points below its cost, it would be sold automatically, thereby limiting the loss to five points.

"'If your commitments are intelligently made in the first place,' the old master continued, 'your profits will average ten, twenty-five, or even fifty points. Consequently, by limiting your losses to five points, you can be wrong more than half of the time and still make plenty of money.'

"I adopted that principle immediately and have used it ever since. It has saved my clients and me many thousands of dollars.

"After a while I realized that the stop-loss principle could be used in other ways besides in the stock market. I began to place stop-loss orders on other worries besides financial ones. I began to place a stop-loss order on any and every kind of annoyance and resentment that came to me. It has worked like magic.

"For example, I often have a luncheon date with a friend who is rarely on time. In the old days, he used to keep me stewing around for half my lunch hour before he showed up. Finally, I told him about my stop-loss orders on my worries. I said, 'Bill, my stop-loss order on waiting for you is exactly ten minutes. If you arrive more than ten minutes late, our luncheon engagement will be sold down the river—and I'll be gone.'"

Man, how I wish I had had the sense, years ago, to put stop-loss orders on my impatience, on my temper, on my desire for self-justification, on my regrets, and on all my mental and emotional strains. Why didn't I have the horse sense to size up each situation that threatened to destroy my peace of mind and say to myself: "See here, Dale Carnegie, this situation is worth just so much fussing about—and no more"? ...Why didn't I?

However, I must give myself credit for a little sense on one occasion, at least. And it was a serious occasion, too—a crisis in my life—when I stood watching my dreams and my plans for the future and the work of years vanish into thin air. It happened like this. In my early thirties, I had decided to spend my life writing novels. I was going to be a second Frank Norris or Jack London or Thomas Hardy. I was so in earnest that I spent two years in Europe—where I could live cheaply with dollars during the period of wild, printing-press money that followed the First World War. I spent two years there, writing my magnum opus. I called it *The Blizzard*. The title was a natural, for the reception it got among publishers was as cold as any blizzard that ever howled across the plains of the Dakotas. When my literary agent told me it was worthless, that I had no gift, no talent, for fiction, my heart almost stopped. I left his office in a daze. I couldn't have been more stunned if he had hit me across the head with a club. I was stupefied. I realized that I was standing at the crossroads of life, and had to make a tremendous decision. What should I do? Which way should I turn? Weeks passed before I came out of the daze.

At that time, I had never heard of the phrase "put a stop-loss order on your worries." But as I look back now, I can see that I did just that. I wrote off my two years of sweating over that novel for just what they were worth—a noble experiment—and went forward from there. I returned to my work of organizing and teaching adult-education classes, and wrote biographies in my spare time—biographies and non-fiction books such as the one you are reading now.

Am I glad now that I made that decision? Glad? Every time I think about it now I feel like dancing in the street for sheer joy!

I honestly believe that one of the greatest secrets to true peace of mind is—a decent sense of values. And I believe we could annihilate fifty percent of all our worries at once if we would develop a sort of private gold standard—a gold standard of what things are worth to us in terms of our lives.

So, to break the worry habit before it breaks you.

Whenever we are tempted to throw good money after bad in terms of human living, let's stop and ask ourselves these three questions:

How much does this thing I am worrying about really matter to me?

At what point shall I set a "stop-loss" order on this worry—and forget it?

Exactly how much shall I pay for this whistle? Have I already paid more than it is worth?

POINTS TO REMEMBER

1. Apply the "stop-loss" principle in the real world.
2. One's moral code determines their attainment of true peace.
3. Break the worry habit before it breaks you.

20

IF YOU MUST FIND FAULT, THIS IS THE WAY TO BEGIN

A friend of mine was a guest at the White House for a weekend during the administration of Calvin Coolidge. Drifting into the President's private office, he heard Coolidge say to one of his secretaries, "That's a very pretty dress you are wearing this morning, and you are a very attractive young woman."

That was probably the most effusive praise Silent Cal had ever bestowed upon a secretary in his life. It was so unusual, so unexpected, that the secretary blushed in confusion. Then Coolidge said, "Now, don't get stuck up. I just said that to make you feel good. From now on, I wish you would be a little more careful with your punctuation."

His method was probably a bit obvious, but the psychology was superb. It is always easier to listen to unpleasant things after we have heard some praise of our good points.

A barber lathers a man before he shaves him; and that is precisely what McKinley did back in 1896, when he was running for President. One of the prominent Republicans of that day had written a campaign speech that he felt was just a trifle better than Cicero and Patrick Henry and Daniel Webster all rolled into one. With great glee, this chap read his immortal speech aloud to McKinley. The speech had its fine points, but it just wouldn't do. McKinley didn't want to hurt the man's feelings. He must not kill the man's splendid enthusiasm, and yet he had to say "no". Note how adroitly he did it.

"My friend, that is a splendid speech, a magnificent speech," McKinley said. "No one could have prepared a better one. There are many occasions on which it would be precisely the right thing to say, but is it quite suitable to this particular occasion? Sound and sober as it is from your standpoint, I must consider its effect from the party's standpoint. Now go home and write a speech along the lines I indicate, and send me a copy of it."

He did just that. McKinley blue-pencilled and helped him rewrite his second speech, and he became one of the effective speakers of the campaign.

Here is the second most famous letter that Abraham Lincoln ever wrote. (His most famous one was written to Mrs. Bixby, expressing his sorrow for the death of the five sons she had lost in battle.) Lincoln probably dashed this letter off in five minutes; yet it sold at public auction in 1926 for $12,000, and that, by the way, was more money than Lincoln was able to save during half a century of hard work. The letter was written to General Joseph Hooker on 26 April 1863, during the darkest period of the Civil War. For eighteen months, Lincoln's generals had been leading the Union Army from one tragic defeat to another. Nothing but futile, stupid human butchery. The nation was appalled. Thousands of soldiers had deserted from the army, and even the Republican members of the Senate had revolted and wanted to force Lincoln out of the White House. "We are now on the brink of destruction," Lincoln said. "It appears to me that even the Almighty is against us. I can hardly see a ray of hope." Such was the period of black sorrow and chaos out of which this letter came.

I am printing the letter here because it shows how Lincoln tried to change an obstreperous general when the very fate of the nation could have depended upon the general's action.

This is perhaps the sharpest letter Abe Lincoln wrote after he became President; yet you will note that he praised General Hooker before he spoke of his grave faults.

Yes, they were grave faults, but Lincoln didn't call them that. Lincoln was more conservative, more diplomatic. Lincoln wrote: "There are some things in regard to which I am not quite satisfied with you." Talk about tact! And diplomacy!

Here is the letter addressed to General Hooker:

> I have placed you at the head of the Army of the Potomac. Of course, I have done this upon what appears to me to be sufficient reasons, and yet I think it best for you to know that there are some things in regard to which I am not quite satisfied with you.
>
> I believe you to be a brave and skillful soldier, which, of course, I like. I also believe you do not mix politics with your profession, in which you are right. You have confidence in yourself, which is a valuable if not an indispensable quality.
>
> You are ambitious, which, within reasonable bounds, does good rather than harm. But I think that during General Burnside's command of the army you have taken counsel of your ambition and thwarted him as much as you could, in which you did a great wrong to the country and to a most meritorious and honourable brother officer.
>
> I have heard, in such a way as to believe it, of your recently saying that both the army and the Government needed a dictator. Of course, it was not for this, but in

> spite of it, that I have given you command.
>
> Only those generals who gain successes can set up as dictators. What I now ask of you is military success and I will risk the dictatorship.
>
> The Government will support you to the utmost of its ability, which is neither more nor less than it has done and will do for all commanders. I much fear that the spirit which you have aided to infuse into the army, of criticising their commander and withholding confidence from him, will now turn upon you. I shall assist you, as far as I can, to put it down.
>
> Neither you nor Napoleon, if he were alive again, could get any good out of an army while such spirit prevails in it, and now beware of rashness. Beware of rashness, but with energy and sleepless vigilance, go forward and give us victories.

You are not a Coolidge, a McKinley or a Lincoln. You want to know whether this philosophy will operate for you in everyday business contacts. Will it? Let's see. Let's take the case of W.P. Gaw, of the Wark Company, Philadelphia.

A PAT ON THE BACK CAN DO WONDERS!

The Wark Company had contracted to build and complete a large office building in Philadelphia by a certain specified date. Everything was going along well; the building was almost finished, when suddenly the subcontractor making the ornamental bronze work to go on the exterior of this building declared that he couldn't make delivery on schedule. What! An entire building held up! Heavy penalties! Distressing losses! All because of one man!

Long-distance telephone calls. Arguments! Heated conversations! All in vain. Then Mr. Gaw was sent to New York to beard the bronze lion in his den.

'Do you know you are the only person in Brooklyn with your name?' Mr. Gaw asked the president of the subcontracting firm shortly after they were introduced. The president was surprised. "No, I didn't know that."

"Well," said Mr. Gaw, "when I got off the train this morning, I looked in the telephone book to get your address, and you're the only person in the Brooklyn phone book with your name."

"I never knew that," the subcontractor said. He checked the phone book with interest. "Well, it's an unusual name," he said proudly. "My family came from Holland and settled in New York almost two hundred years ago." He continued to talk about his family and his ancestors for several minutes. When he finished that, Mr. Gaw complimented him on how large a plant he had and compared it favorably with a number of similar plants he had visited. "It is one of the cleanest and neatest bronze factories I ever saw," said Gaw.

"I've spent a lifetime building up this business," the subcontractor said, "and I am rather proud of it. Would you like to take a look around the factory?"

During this tour of inspection, Mr. Gaw complimented the other man on his system of fabrication and told him how and why it seemed superior to those of some of his competitors. Gaw commented on some unusual machines, and the subcontractor announced that he himself had invented those machines. He spent considerable time showing Gaw how they operated and the superior work they turned out. He insisted on taking his visitor to lunch. So far, mind you, not a word had been said about the real purpose of Gaw's visit.

After lunch, the subcontractor said, "Now, to get down

to business. Naturally, I know why you're here. I didn't expect that our meeting would be so enjoyable. You can go back to Philadelphia with my promise that your material will be fabricated and shipped, even if other orders have to be delayed."

Mr. Gaw got everything that he wanted without even asking for it. The material arrived on time, and the building was completed on the day the completion contract specified.

Would this have happened had Mr. Gaw used the hammer-and-dynamite method generally employed on such occasions?

Dorothy Wrublewski, a branch manager of the Fort Monmouth, New Jersey, Federal Credit Union, reported to one of our classes how she was able to help one of her employees become more productive.

"We recently hired a young lady as a teller trainee. Her contact with our customers was very good. She was accurate and efficient in handling individual transactions. The problem developed at the end of the day when it was time to balance out.

"The head teller came to me and strongly suggested that I fire this woman. 'She is holding up everyone else because she is so slow in balancing out. I've shown her over and over, but she can't get it. She's got to go.'

"The next day I observed her working quickly and accurately when handling the normal everyday transactions, and she was very pleasant with our customers.

"It didn't take long to discover why she had trouble balancing out. After the office closed, I went over to talk with her. She was obviously nervous and upset. I praised her for being so friendly and outgoing with the customers and complimented her for the accuracy and speed used in that work. I then suggested we review the procedure we use in balancing the cash drawer. Once she realized I had confidence in her, she easily followed my suggestions and soon mastered this function. We have had no problems with her since then.'

POINTS TO REMEMBER

1. It is always easier to listen to unpleasant things after we have heard some praise of our good points.
2. There are a thousand ways to say "no".
3. Your trust is the best gift you can give to someone.

21

TALK ABOUT YOUR OWN MISTAKES FIRST

Admitting one's own mistakes—even when one hasn't corrected them—can help convince somebody to change his behaviour. This was illustrated more recently by Clarence Zerhusen of Timonium, Maryland, when he discovered his fifteen-year-old son was experimenting with cigarettes.

"Naturally, I didn't want David to smoke," Mr. Zerhusen told us, "but his mother and I smoked cigarettes; we were giving him a bad example all the time. I explained to Dave how I started smoking at about his age and how the nicotine had gotten the best of me and now it was nearly impossible for me to stop. I reminded him how irritating my cough was and how he had been after me to give up cigarettes not many years before.

"I didn't exhort him to stop or make threats or warn him about their dangers. All I did was point out how I was hooked on cigarettes and what it had meant to me.

"He thought about it for a while and decided he wouldn't smoke until he had graduated from high school. As the years went by David never did start smoking and has no intention of ever doing so.

"As a result of that conversation I made the decision to stop smoking cigarettes myself, and with the support of my family, I have succeeded."

A good leader follows this principle:

BEFORE CRITICIZING THE OTHER PERSON, TALK ABOUT YOUR OWN MISTAKES.

POINTS TO REMEMBER

1. To be able to criticize and not be hated for it, speak about your mistakes first.
2. Good leadership is to correct your subordinates without lowering their morale.
3. Sharing responsibility with others for their errors strengthens relationships.

22

HOW TO CRITICIZE—AND NOT BE HATED FOR IT

Many people begin their criticism with sincere praise followed by the word "but" and ending with a critical statement. For example, in trying to change a child's careless attitude toward studies, we might say, "We're really proud of you, Johnnie, for raising your grades this term. *But* if you had worked harder on your algebra, the results would have been better."

In this case, Johnnie might feel encouraged until he heard the word "but". He might then question the sincerity of the original praise. To him, the praise seemed only to be a contrived lead-in to a critical inference of failure. Credibility would be strained, and we probably would not achieve our objectives of changing Johnnie's attitude toward his studies.

This could be easily overcome by changing the word "but" to "and". "We're really proud of you, Johnnie, for raising your grades this term, *and* by continuing the same conscientious efforts next term, your algebra grade can be up with all the others."

Now, Johnnie would accept the praise because there was no follow-up of an inference of failure. We have called his attention to the behaviour we wished to change indirectly, and the chances are he will try to live up to our expectations.

Calling attention to one's mistakes indirectly works wonders with sensitive people who may resent bitterly any direct criticism. Marge Jacob of Woonsocket, Rhode Island, told one of our classes how she convinced some sloppy construction workers to clean up after themselves when they were building additions to her house.

For the first few days of the work, when Mrs. Jacob returned from her job, she noticed that the yard was strewn with the cut ends of lumber. She didn't want to antagonize the builders, because they did excellent work. So after the workers had gone home, she and her children picked up and neatly piled all the lumber debris in a corner. The following morning she called the foreman to one side and said, "I'm really pleased with the way the front lawn was left last night; it is nice and clean and does not offend the neighbors." From that day forward the workers picked up and piled the debris to one side, and the foreman came in each day seeking approval of the condition the lawn was left in after a day's work.

One of the major areas of controversy between members of the army reserves and their regular army trainers is haircuts. The reservists consider themselves civilians (which they are most of the time) and resent having to cut their hair short.

Master Sergeant Harley Kaiser of the 542nd USAR School addressed himself to this problem when he was working with a group of reserve non-commissioned officers. As an old-time regular-army master sergeant, he might have been expected to yell at his troops and threaten them. Instead he chose to make his point indirectly.

"Gentlemen," he started, "you are leaders. You will be most effective when you lead by example. You must be the example for your men to follow. You know what the army regulations say about haircuts. I am going to get my hair cut today, although it is still much shorter than some of yours. You look at yourself in the mirror, and if you feel you need a haircut to be a good example, we'll arrange time for you to visit the post barbershop."

The result was predictable. Several of the candidates did look in the mirror and went to the barbershop that afternoon and received "regulation" haircuts. Sergeant Kaiser commented the next morning that he already could see the development of leadership qualities in some of the members of the squad.

On 8 March 1887, the eloquent Henry Ward Beecher died. The following Sunday, Lyman Abbott was invited to speak in the pulpit left silent by Beecher's passing. Eager to do his best, he wrote, rewrote and polished his sermon with the meticulous care of a Flaubert. Then he read it to his wife. It was poor—as most written speeches are. She might have said, if she had had less judgement, "Lyman, that is terrible. That'll never do. You'll put people to sleep. It reads like an encyclopedia. You ought to know better than that after all the years you have been preaching. For heaven's sake, why don't you talk like a human being? Why don't you act natural? You'll disgrace yourself if you ever read that stuff."

That's what she *might* have said. And, if she had, you know what would have happened. And she knew too. So, she merely remarked that it would make an excellent article for the *North American Review*. In other words, she praised it and at the same time subtly suggested that it wouldn't do as a speech. Lyman Abbott saw the point, tore up his carefully prepared manuscript and preached without even using notes.

POINTS TO REMEMBER

1. Modify your vocabulary to soften the blow of criticism.
2. Never directly address someone's error.
3. If you have to criticize once, praise thrice.

23

A DROP OF HONEY

If your temper is aroused and you tell 'em a thing or two, you will have a fine time unloading your feelings. But what about the other person? Will he share your pleasure? Will your belligerent tones, your hostile attitude, make it easy for him to agree with you?

"If you come at me with your fists doubled," said Woodrow Wilson, "I think I can promise you that mine will double as fast as yours; but if you come to me and say, 'Let us sit down and take counsel together, and, if we differ from each other, understand why it is that we differ, just what the points at issue are,' we will presently find that we are not so far apart after all, that the points on which we differ are few and the points on which we agree are many, and that if we only have the patience and the candour and the desire to get together, we will get together."

Nobody appreciated the truth of Woodrow Wilson's statement more than John D. Rockefeller Jr. Back in 1915, Rockefeller was the most fiercely despised man in Colorado. One of the bloodiest strikes in the history of American industry had been shocking the state for two terrible years. Irate, belligerent miners were demanding higher wages from the Colorado Fuel and Iron Company; Rockefeller controlled that company. Property had been destroyed, troops had been called out. Blood had been shed. Strikers had been shot, their bodies riddled with bullets.

At a time like that, with the air seething with hatred, Rockefeller wanted to win the strikers to his way of thinking. And he did it. How? Here's the story. After weeks spent in making friends, Rockefeller addressed the representatives of the strikers. This speech, in its entirety, is a masterpiece. It produced astonishing results. It calmed the tempestuous waves of hate that threatened to engulf Rockefeller. It won him a host of admirers. It presented facts in such a friendly manner that the strikers went back to work without saying another word about the increase in wages for which they had fought so violently.

The opening of that remarkable speech follows. Note how it fairly glows with friendliness. Rockefeller, remember, was talking to men who, a few days previously, had wanted to hang him by the neck to a sour apple tree; yet he couldn't have been more gracious, more friendly if he had addressed a group of medical missionaries. His speech was radiant with such phrases as I am *proud* to be here, having *visited* in *your homes*, met many of your wives and children, we meet here not as strangers, but *as friends*...spirit of *mutual friendship*, our *common interests*, it is only by *your courtesy* that I am here.

"This is a red-letter day in my life," Rockefeller began. "It is the first time I have ever had the good fortune to meet the representatives of the employees of this great company, its officers and superintendents, together, and I can assure you that I am proud to be here, and that I shall remember this gathering as long as I live. Had this meeting been held two weeks ago, I should have stood here a stranger to most of you, recognizing a few faces, I having had the opportunity last week of visiting all the camps in the southern coal field and of talking individually with practically all of the representatives, except those who were away; having visited in your homes, met many of your wives and children, we meet here not as strangers, but as friends, and it is in that spirit of mutual friendship that I am glad to have this opportunity to discuss with you our common interests.

"Since this is a meeting of the officers of the company and the representatives of the employees, it is only by your courtesy that I am here, for I am not so fortunate as to be either one or the other; and yet I feel that I am intimately associated with you men, for, in a sense, I represent both the stockholders and the directors."

Isn't that a superb example of the fine art of making friends out of enemies?

Suppose Rockefeller had taken a different tack. Suppose he had argued with those miners and hurled devastating facts in their faces. Suppose he had told them by his tones and insinuations that they were wrong. Suppose that, by all the rules of logic, he had proved that they were wrong. What would have happened? More anger would have been stirred up, more hatred, more revolt.

If a man's heart is ranking with discord and ill feeling toward you, you can't win him to your way of thinking with all the logic in Christendom. Scolding parents and domineering bosses and husbands and nagging wives ought to realise that people don't want to change their minds. They can't be forced or driven to agree with you or me. But they may possibly be led to, if we are gentle and friendly, ever so gentle and ever so friendly.

Lincoln said that, in effect, over a hundred years ago. Here are his words:

> It is an old and true maxim that "a drop of honey catches more flies than a gallon of gall." So with men, if you

> would win a man to your cause, first convince him that you are his sincere friend. Therein is a drop of honey that catches his heart; which, say what you will, is the great high road to his reason.

Business executives have learnt that it pays to be friendly to strikers. For example, when 2,500 employees in the White Motor Company's plant struck for higher wages and a union shop, Robert F. Black, then president of the company, didn't lose his temper and condemn and threaten and talk of tyranny and Communists. He actually praised the strikers. He published an advertisement in the Cleveland papers, complimenting them on "the peaceful way in which they laid down their tools." Finding the strike pickets idle, he bought them a couple of dozen baseball bats and gloves and invited them to play ball on vacant lots. For those who preferred bowling, he rented a bowling alley.

This friendliness on Mr. Black's part did what friendliness always does: it begot friendliness. So the strikers borrowed brooms, shovels and rubbish carts, and began picking up matches, papers, cigarette stubs and cigar butts around the factory. Imagine it! Imagine strikers tidying up the factory grounds while battling for higher wages and recognition of the union. Such an event had never been heard of before in the long, tempestuous history of American labour wars. That strike ended with a compromise settlement within a week—ended without any ill feeling or rancour.

HOW TO HANDLE FAILURES

Years ago, when I was a barefoot boy walking through the woods to a country school out in northwest Missouri, I read a fable about the sun and the wind. They quarrelled about which was the stronger, and the wind said, "I'll prove I am. See the old man down there with a coat? I bet I can get his coat off him quicker than you can."

So the sun went behind a cloud, and the wind blew until it was almost a tornado, but the harder it blew, the tighter the old man clutched his coat to him.

Finally, the wind calmed down and gave up, and then the sun came out from behind the clouds and smiled kindly on the old man. Presently, he mopped his brow and pulled off his coat. The sun then told the wind that gentleness and friendliness were always stronger than fury and force.

The use of gentleness and friendliness is demonstrated day after day by people who have learnt that a drop of honey catches more flies than a gallon of gall. Aesop was a Greek slave who lived at the court of Croesus and spun immortal fables 600 years before Christ. Yet the truths he taught about human nature are just as true in Boston and Birmingham now as they were 26 centuries ago in Athens. The sun can make you take off your coat more quickly than the wind; and kindliness, the friendly approach and appreciation can make people change their minds more readily than all the bluster and storming in the world.

Remember what Lincoln said: "A drop of honey catches more flies than a gallon of gall."

POINTS TO REMEMBER

1. Learn the art of making friends out of enemies.
2. The most appreciated speech is one which is friendly in its tone.
3. A drop of honey catches more flies than a gallon of gall.